Teach Like Jesus

By Josh Hunt

If you enjoy these this book, you might check out the thousands of lessons available at a low subscription price at

http://mybiblestudylessons.com/

Contents

Tell lots of stories .1

Expect people to change 21

Ask lots of questions 35

Confront 51

Hands-on 65

Love Like Jesus 85

Intriguing 101

Kid-friendly 127

Example 137

Just teach 147

Easy to understand; impossible to fathom . . 153

Send them out to do 161

Unexpected 175

Slogans 189

Conclusion 201

Note

Thanks to the following people for reading early drafts of this book and offering suggestions:

David Haskins
Joel Beck
Michael Tollett
Delton Frost
Missy Hunt
JD Templeton
Mark Mullins
Esther Purkey
Jim O'Dillon
Derick Dickens
Richard Sargent
Steve North
Charles Wallis
Jim Monroe
Ken Row
John Ambra
George Quesenberry
Harold Phillips
Cindy Jo Booth
Mark Mullins
James Lyons

Greg Fisher
Kathy Weiser
Tom Farr
Diane Courville

About the Author

Josh Hunt is the author of numerous books, including...

Disciplemaking Teachers
The Effective Bible Teacher
Good Questions Have Groups Talking
You Can Double Your Class in Two Years or Less
Doubling Groups 2.0
You Can Double Your Church in Five Years or Less
Break a Habit; Make a Habit
How to Get Along with Almost Anyone
and, hundreds and hundreds of Bible studies in the series, Good Questions Have Groups Talking

Josh's main job is writing Bible Study lessons. He publishes these in book form (available on Amazon) and as part of the Good Questions Have Groups Talking subscription service.
Like Netflix for Bible lessons, it gives teachers access to Bible lessons on every book of the Bible and every topic imaginable. Each Lesson consists of about 20 ready-to-use questions, as well as answers from well-known authors and

commentators. For more information, see https://www.mybiblestudylessons.com/

Josh lives in Las Cruces, NM. He pastors a small church in the country. He enjoys hiking and spending time with family. His hobbies include hiking, photography and playing keyboard.

Commendations

No one ever taught like Jesus. When we learn from Him we truly are learning from the Master Teacher. Josh Hunt is uniquely qualified to help us teach like Jesus because these are the practices he has personally used for years! Anyone who wants to become a better teacher must have this book!

Allan Taylor

Author, *Sunday School in HD*

I have had the pleasure of hearing Josh teach this material in person and I can assure you that it always has an impact on the audience. It is both entertaining and informative. It will challenge you to communicate more effectively. It is biblically based and practically oriented. Your teaching will be improved if you follow the suggestions included in these pages. Here's the good news. The book is as entertaining and informative as the live presentation! Buy it! Read it! Teach like Jesus!

Ken Hemphill

Director of Church Planting and Revitalization Center

North Greenville University

If you want to be the best teacher you can possibly be, *Teach Like Jesus*. That is not only a wonderful title for a book on how to teach, that is the secret to becoming the greatest teacher you can become. Anyone who wants to have a greater ministry in teaching should read this book.
Elmer Towns
Co-Founder, Liberty University
Lynchburg, Virginia

When it comes to teaching the Bible, nobody knows his stuff any better than Josh Hunt. Josh's new book, *Teach Like Jesus*, is a must read for every pastor, Sunday School director, minister of education, and Sunday School teacher out there. Josh combines years of experience, biblical analysis, and spiritual insight to provide a resource for teachers in the 21st century. But Teach Like Jesus is not just a book about theory. Woven throughout the book are practical ideas of how to put concept into reality.
Bob Mayfield
Sunday School and Discipleship
Baptist General Convention of Oklahoma

I read everything Josh has to say about teaching, group life and discipleship. This is his very best! Every member of our staff will be reading this and I am planning to get a copy for the majority of our volunteer teachers. It will make them better! Josh provides literally hundreds of applicable ideas, reminders, tips and "how-to's" to help your teaching be "the best"!
Jeff Young
Prestonwood Church,
Dallas, TX

"Josh has done it again! He has written a book that will cause the church to rethink the way we make disciples. Josh understands how to equip teachers not with educational theory, but with the practical and proven skills used by Jesus. This is a must read for all those who teach or preach."
Dr. Chad Keck
Author, *Ordinarily Faithful: Life Lessons From the Judges: Gideon*

If you teach Sunday school or lead a small group, this book will help you. It doesn't matter what age group you teach because Jesus taught the young and the old.

Jesus is our example for living and His teaching methods should be our goal as teachers. The way Jesus taught changed lives so our teaching needs to produce life change as well.

Josh is a gifted leader that has provided us with a resource to assist us in following Jesus as our master teacher.

Dr. Tim S. Smith, State Missionary
Sunday School & Small Groups Specialist
Georgia Baptist Convention

Introduction

It is not enough to teach *what* Jesus taught; we must teach *how* Jesus taught. Jesus taught in such a way as to turn the world upside down.

Jesus didn't have an outreach program. He didn't do marketing. He didn't contact absentees. He didn't seem to worry about attendance. And yet they came. Boy, did they come.

I have spent the last twelve years crisscrossing the country telling groups how they can double every two years or less. Occasionally, I visit classes. Often, they are good, but all too often it doesn't take too much effort to see why Sunday School is failing—and this is a problem an outreach program will not solve. They are failing because the teaching is crummy. It is nowhere close to what I describe in *You Can Double Your Class in Two Years or Less* as "half-way decent teaching." It is in a different time zone from the teaching of Jesus.

This book is an effort to examine the teaching
style of Jesus with a view to helping teachers
teach more like Jesus. Who wouldn't want that?

Tell lots of stories

Who is the greatest teacher that ever lived? (It is a book on teaching like Jesus; take a guess!) And how did Jesus teach? He told lots of stories.

The Bible calls them parables—which gives us the idea that this is some special kind of spiritual story. Curious thing about that word parable: it is not really a translation of the Greek word. It is a transliteration. A translation is where we take the Greek word and translate it into English. A transliteration is where we take each Greek letter and turn it into an English letter. The Greek word for parable is parabolé. If we were to actually translate it, we would translate it with the word "story." This is in fact how the New Living translates the word half the time. Here is the breakdown of how the word is translated in the NLT:[1]

---

[1] Copyright Faithlife Corporation, makers of Logos Bible Software – www.logos.com

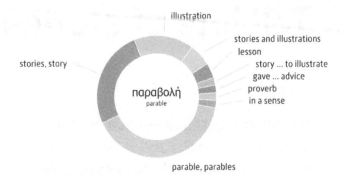

Of course, we have gained a good English word in the process: parable, which is an equally good translation.

Perhaps you are thinking: OK, I knew that, Jesus spoke in parables. Tell me something I didn't know. Here is a verse you might have missed:

> *Matthew 13:34 (NIV) Jesus spoke all these things to the crowd in parables; he did not say anything to them without using a parable.*

I love the way the Message has it. A little loose with the text, to be sure, but it sure makes the passage come alive:

> *Matthew 13:34 (MSG) All Jesus did that day was tell stories—a long storytelling afternoon.*

Here is the principle: anytime we do a teaching and don't include a generous helping of stories we fail to teach like Jesus.

Which is easier to remember?

One of my favorite books on teaching is *Made to Stick* by Heath and Heath. They illustrate the power of story by telling this one:[2]

> A friend of a friend of ours is a frequent business traveler. Let's call him Dave. Dave was recently in Atlantic City for an important meeting with clients. Afterward, he had some time to kill before his flight, so he went to a local bar for a drink.
>
> He'd just finished one drink when an attractive woman approached and asked if she could buy him another. He was surprised but flattered. Sure, he said. The woman walked to the bar and brought back two more drinks—one for her and one for him. He thanked her and took a sip. And that was the last thing he remembered.
>
> Rather, that was the last thing he remembered until he woke up, disoriented, lying in a hotel bathtub, his body submerged in ice.

---

[2] Heath, Chip; Heath, Dan (2007-01-02). *Made to Stick: Why Some Ideas Survive and Others Die* (Kindle Locations 50-64). Random House. Kindle Edition.

He looked around frantically, trying to figure out where he was and how he got there. Then he spotted the note:

DON'T MOVE. CALL 911.

A cell phone rested on a small table beside the bathtub. He picked it up and called 911, his fingers numb and clumsy from the ice. The operator seemed oddly familiar with his situation. She said, "Sir, I want you to reach behind you, slowly and carefully. Is there a tube protruding from your lower back?"

Anxious, he felt around behind him. Sure enough, there was a tube.

The operator said, "Sir, don't panic, but one of your kidneys has been harvested. There's a ring of organ thieves operating in this city, and they got to you. Paramedics are on their way. Don't move until they arrive."

Call a friend. See if you can tell them this story from memory. Now; contrast that with this piece:[3]

"Comprehensive community building naturally lends itself to a return-on-investment rationale that can be modeled, drawing on existing practice," it begins, going on to argue that "[a] factor constraining the flow of resources to CCIs is that funders must often resort to

---

[3] Heath, Chip; Heath, Dan (2007-01-02). *Made to Stick: Why Some Ideas Survive and Others Die* (Kindle Locations 76-79). Random House. Kindle Edition.

targeting or categorical requirements in grant making to ensure accountability."

Imagine you were to call a friend and try to recall that. Stories stick to the brain. But why?

Why are stories so effective?

Modern brain research has confirmed what teachers have long known: stories stick to the brain. As one writer put it: "We think in story. It's hardwired in our brain."[4] The question is why? Why do stories stick to the brain? Why is the brain "Teflon" when it comes to remembering almost everything and Velcro to remembering a good story?

Picture the mind like a fort. Your job as a teacher is to get your information past the gate. The ego pushes the doors closed, keeping everything out. The ego doesn't think it needs any information. It certainly doesn't think it needs to change in any way. The ego diligently guards against any outside information coming in—particularly convicting or life-changing information.

---

[4] Cron, Lisa (2012-07-10). *Wired for Story: The Writer's Guide to Using Brain Science to Hook Readers from the Very First Sentence* (Kindle Location 179). Random House, Inc.. Kindle Edition.

How do you get the ego to relax and quit pushing against the door? Distract him. Tell him a story. Get him thinking about something else. He gets so caught up in the story that he forgets about pushing the door closed. The door swings open and your information gets through.

The classic example of this is the story of Nathan confronting David the king. People got their heads chopped off back in the day for confronting the king. People got their heads lopped off for being in a bad mood in front of the king. How does Nathan confront David the king? He tells a story. The story is so masterfully told that David forgets all about himself (this is often hard to do). He gets all fired up about the injustice in this story.

2 Samuel 12.5 records that David was hot. Look at how the various translations treat this phrase:

- 2 Samuel 12:5 (NIV) David burned with anger against the man.
- 2 Samuel 12:5 (CEV) David was furious.
- 2 Samuel 12:5 (ESV) Then David's anger was greatly kindled against the man.
- 2 Samuel 12:5 (HCSB) David was infuriated.
- 2 Samuel 12:5 (MSG) David exploded in anger.
- 2 Samuel 12:5 (NKJV) So David's anger was greatly aroused.

David was so caught up in his own anger that he didn't realize that Nathan was talking about him. The light came on when Nathan said four words: "You are the man."

Jesus often used this approach with the Pharisees. I don't think they saw themselves as the elder brother until the very end of the story.

What makes a good story?

Stories can be long or short. They can be a sentence or a novel. If they are a sentence, there are not a lot of rules. The longer the story is, the more difficult it is to stay interesting. If you tell a long story, make sure it has these elements:

- **A mountain to climb, a river to cross, a battle to fight, a love to win**. There needs to be some cause. The more important the cause the better the story. This is what makes the gospel such a good story: God is saving the world. If it is a story about how you want to buy a cool car just because you think it is cool, it might not be all that great of a story. The bigger the mountain, the better the story. This is why there are so many movies about some natural or man-made disaster that will wipe out planet earth.

- **Character development.** The longer the story goes, the more we want to get to know the personality and quirks of the characters. People love hearing about people. That's what makes magazines like, *People* so interesting to many. From one perspective, the hill to climb is not really the story. The way that climbing the hill changes the main characters is the real story.
- **An uh-oh**. In a good story things start out looking impossible. Then things get worse. Just when you thought the mountain was impossible to climb, the hero loses his oxygen. Now it seems totally impossible.

Consider the story of Jesus healing Jairus' daughter. There is a mountain to climb: Jairus' daughter is sick. The hill to climb in this story is an important one. Who can't relate to the compassion of a dad for his daughter? Then, there is an uh-oh. She dies. Now things look utterly impossible. Luke 8.53 says they laughed at him when he said she was merely sleeping.

The ultimate example of what appeared to be an uh-oh is the cross. Jesus came to save the world. Then he gets killed. Uh-oh. How is this going to work out? What a great story!

- **The twist.** It is always great when there is something unexpected in the story. We love a story we can't predict. If you can predict the outcome, why bother paying attention?

Consider the story of the wedding feast told in Matthew 22. A king gave a wedding feast for his son. He wanted the place packed with people. Apparently the king wasn't very well-liked because he was having a hard time getting people to show up. That is the mountain to climb—getting people to show up. Eventually he invites enough people that the place is full. (He has to employ some very persuasive methods to get people to come.) Here is the twist. One guy even got in without his wedding garment. Everyone gasps. He is kicked out on his ear. No one saw that coming.

- **The triumph of the glorious ending.** The hero makes it to the top after all.
- **The wind down.** Watch any good movie and it will have this pattern. There is always a wind down after the mountain is conquered.

Where to find good stories

Good stories can be found everywhere. The key is to start looking early. As soon as one lesson is over, start preparing for the next. Don't wait until the day before. Give yourself lots of time to find great stories. Every book you read, every movie you watch and every conversation you engage in will help you prepare if you know what the topic is early in the week. Here is a short list of places to find good stories:

The Bible.

By telling stories from the Bible, you let the stories do double duty. They make the point you are trying to make, and, they also teach the Bible. Include lots of stories from the Bible. When you want to make a point, ask first: Can I think of a biblical story to illustrate this?

- Teaching on being critical? Tell the story of Miriam and Aaron criticizing Moses.
- Teaching on kindness? Teach about David's kindness to Mephibosheth.
- Teaching on Romans 8.28? Tell the story of Joseph.
- Need an example of a leader? Look no further than Nehemiah.

Personal stories

Stories from your own life are great as long as they are not overdone. People want the teachers to be self-disclosing. They want to get to know you as well as the Bible. But, it is not all about you. Personal stories can be overdone. Want a rule of thumb? Somewhere in the range of 10% of your stories ought to be about you. If you don't ever include stories about yourself you come across as distant and aloof. People want to know how Christianity really works in your life. It is not all principles and concepts. It is personal. But, it is not all about you.

Observation of life

You can find lots of stories simply by observing the world around you.

This poor widow. . .

Jesus told this story simply by observing the world around him:

> As Jesus looked up, he saw the rich putting their gifts into the temple treasury. He also saw a poor widow put in two very small copper coins. "Truly I tell you," he said, "this poor widow has put in more than all the others. All these people gave their gifts out of their wealth; but she out of her poverty put in all she had to live on." Luke 21:1–4 (NIV)

Jesus could have made this point simply by making it—simply by giving a talk on *The Three Principles of Giving*. Jesus the Teacher knew it was more interesting to tell a story. The story was not abstract and separated from life. It was a day-to-day slice of life experience. It was a simple observation of what he saw in the world around them. This observation could have been made by any of his listeners. It was not particularly dramatic or funny or touching. It was a simple observation of life.

There is a nice thing about a story like this. People would be reminded of it every time they went to the temple. Every time they saw those "trumpets," as they were called—where people placed their offerings—they would be reminded of this woman who gave a "lepton." Literally the word means, "thin one" and it was one-fortieth of a new penny. Jesus valued it greatly. The disciples would never forget.

Teach like Jesus.

One more thing: notice that Jesus taught out of his day-to-day life. Teachers tend to tell too many stories about things that happened twenty years ago. Your group is wondering, "Has Jesus done anything for you lately?" Tell stories that come out of your life this week. Jesus did. Teach like Jesus.

This is not to say we should never use old stories. Jesus said, "Therefore every teacher of the law who has been instructed about the kingdom of heaven is like the owner of a house who brings out of his storeroom new treasures as well as old." Matthew 13:52 (NIV)

Some stories are timeless. They are classic. They are once in a lifetime. When I talk on giving Friday nights to Jesus I often tell the story of the first time we gave Friday nights to Jesus. There is nothing like the first time. But I do well to talk about my life now as well. If all my stories are of practicing hospitality twenty years ago, people will get the idea that it is something I used to do but don't believe in it any more.

I actually have a new plan for my life around hospitality. God has placed me in a church with a bunch of farmers who play a domino game called 42. Know anyone who plays 42? I didn't think so. But, guess who else plays 42? Me. We grew up playing 42 on the mission field in the Philippines. We didn't have much TV available and I think I went to two movies before I started Junior High. So, to entertain ourselves, the family played 42. What a coincidence that a 42 playing pastor would end up with a 42 playing people. It is almost like God has something to do with it. Well, I can take a hint. Perhaps God wants me to offer hospitality by playing 42 with my folks. That is my new plan for my life.

Pause.

Evaluate your level of interest right now. Is a current story of what God is currently doing in my life more interesting than a 20-year-old story?

Story-rich books

I love reading books by people like John Ortberg, Max Lucado and Charles Swindoll that include plenty of good stories. I'd encourage you to read in these books regularly. Subscribe to good podcasts so you are hearing good sermons that include good stories.

By the way, if you read books on a Kindle, you make finding stories a whole lot easier. I was recently doing a lesson on Jehoshaphat. A quick search on the Kindle revealed some great stories I could include in the Good Question lesson I was writing.

Illustration books and websites

www.sermoncentral.com is one source of good stories. Go to any Christian book store and you will find books full of illustrations. One nice thing about the sermoncentral site is that you can search by biblical text, topic, or type of illustration. If you want a humorous story related to Psalms 23 you can find it there. You can also add illustrations to the list, or edit the topic and texts of ones that are there. You can add star ratings so the good ones will float to the top. What a time to be alive.

The news

Generally speaking, most sermons have too many stories from the farm and not enough stories from the news. We sometimes sound like we are from a different time in history. If you want to sound current, tell current stories from current events, the news and pop-culture. Here is one site that features fresh illustrations straight from the headlines: http://www.freshsermonillustrations.net/

Consider Jesus' words in Luke 13:4 (NIV), "Or those eighteen who died when the tower in Siloam fell on them—do you think they were more guilty than all the others living in Jerusalem?" He could have just taught the principle: bad things happen to good people. That is how life is on planet earth. Accept it; deal with it.

The Master Teacher knew it is better to teach with story. Better to give an example. A story doesn't have to be long. This is a one sentence story—a reference to a story that they all knew.

By using a story from the news, as Jesus does here, you save some time. You don't have to tell the whole story because people already know the story. All you have to do is reference it.

We don't know any more about this story than what is said here. But, you get the impression that this story is from the daily news. It is current. Because preachers tend to read old books of sermons, we tend to have lots of stories in our sermons about the farm. Not many of us live on the farm. We need more stories from the city and fewer from the farm. We need more stories from the news and fewer from the history books.

Jesus taught in a way that was current. He didn't sound old fashioned or out of touch. He told stories from the day-to-day lives that people lived in.

Teach like Jesus.

The news broke this week about Arnold Schwarzenegger's love child. This week I was preparing a message on Peter denying Christ. Arnold's story made a perfect introduction. I put his photo on the opening PowerPoint slide and asked, "Why was this man in the news this week? What was it about what he did that bothered us so?" Not only did he have an affair. Not only did he father a child. But he kept it a secret. He kept it secret for 10 years. That is what bugs us. We hate people who live a double life.

It bugged Jesus too. Bugged is too mild a word. Jesus reserved his strongest rebuke for the Pharisees. Jesus' accusation against the Pharisees was that they were hypocritical. They pretended to be something they were not. We hate people like that. We hate people who are nice to us when we are together and say bad things when we are not around. We want people to be consistent.

This is what bugs us about what Peter did. He wasn't consistent. When he was with Jesus he was all smiles and promises. He promised to be true blue faithful to the end. When the heat was on, Peter denied he even knew Christ—not once, but three times.

Arnold was the perfect introduction to this idea because it was current and it fit perfectly around the idea that we want people to be consistent and hate it when they are hypocritical.

New and old

There are not many verses where Jesus actually explains how to be a good teacher. He models great teaching, but he doesn't tell us how to be an effective teacher. Matthew 13:52 is an exception: "And he said to them, "Therefore every scribe who has been trained for the kingdom of heaven is like a master of a house, who brings out of his treasure what is new and what is old." Matthew 13:52 (ESV)

What do we learn about good teaching from this passage? Well, I think there are several applications:

- The effective teacher uses old stories as well as new. In my experience, most preachers have too many old stories. We ought to have some old stories but the scribe trained for the kingdom of heaven brings out new ones as well.
- New and Old can refer to Old Testament stories as well as New Testament parables.

- Effective teachers talk about what God has done in their lives recently, as well as what happened a long time ago. It is great that God saved you and worked in your life 20 years ago. Have you learned anything lately?
- Some new churches try so hard to be current they err in the opposite direction. They never quote from Spurgeon or Wesley or Whitefield. Preachers who do this are cutting people off from a tremendous wealth of insight. Effective teachers bring insight new and old.

Good Questions have groups talking

What if you had a personal research assistant that could find stories for you? What if this someone had access to hundreds of commentaries, illustration books, theology books as well as trade books by popular authors like Maxwell, Swindoll, Stanley, Lucado, Moore, and Piper.

I'd like to be your research assistant. I spend about 20 hours a week writing Good Questions Have Groups Talking. Each lesson consists of about 20 questions that get groups talking. I provide answers in the form of excerpts from the great commentaries, as well as stories and illustrations from great books. For less than the cost of a cup of coffee a week, you can be provided with a steady stream of great stories. Lessons correspond with Lifeway's outlines as well as the International Standard Series. There are lessons on every book of the Bible and every topic imaginable.

See https://www.mybiblestudylessons.com/

Expect people to change

There has been a good deal of research around the idea that a teacher's expectation of the student has a lot to do with the student's performance. Teachers who think their students are smart tend to produce smart students. The converse is also true. Here is how one researcher put it: [5]

> Simply put, when teachers expect students to do well and show intellectual growth, they do; when teachers do not have such expectations, performance and growth are not so encouraged and may in fact be discouraged in a variety of ways. In the famous Oak School experiment, teachers were led to believe that certain students selected at random were likely to be showing signs of a spurt in intellectual growth and development. At the end of the year, the students of whom the teachers had these expectations showed significantly greater gains in intellectual growth than did those in the control group.

This research has a name: The Pygmalion Effect. Pygmalion is named after the ancient Greek story

---

[5] http://www.ntlf.com/html/pi/9902/pygm_1.htm

by Ovid. In the story Pygmalion carves a woman out of ivory and falls in love with her. He asks that the gods bring her to life and eventually they do. His love for her causes her to come to life. A teacher's love for and belief in their students causes them to come to life. Bruce Wilkinson puts it this way: "The influence of our expectations is incredible, a gift from the Lord that should be consciously utilized for the good of our students and family."[6]

The effect is not limited to the classroom: [7]

> *Researchers at Tel Aviv University have found that employee performance in the workplace, like students' grades at school, is greatly influenced by managers' expectations of that performance.*
>
> *An analysis of results from twenty-five years' worth of experimental research conducted at banks, schools, the Israel Defense Forces -- and even summer camp -- shows unequivocal results: when a leader expects subordinates to perform well, they do.*

I consider Bruce Wilkinson's *Seven Laws of the Learner* video series the best teacher training on the planet. It ought to be a required course for

[6] Wilkinson, Bruce (2010). *The Seven Laws of the Learner: How to Teach Almost Anything to Practically Anyone* (p. 90). Multnomah Books. Kindle Edition.

[7] http://www.aftau.org/site/News2?page=NewsArticle&id=6927

every teacher. He tells a fascinating story about being assigned the Section Two group his first year as a professor. What was a Section Two group? Bruce didn't know until a fellow professor explained it to him.[8]

> "Section two has all the top high school seniors coming into the freshman class. The honors group. Cream of the crop. The most outstanding group of students in the whole college."

> "Motivation! Like a team of wild horses straining at the reins. Those kids'll just pull it out of you."

Bruce goes on to describe the exhilarating experience of working with these race horse students. And it wasn't all subjective. He pulls out a stack of ungraded papers—one from Section One, one from Section Two and one from Section Three. The Section Two group wrote more pages than the other two groups combined. The grades in Section Two were substantially better.

Then Bruce learns the shocker. They had done away with the Section Two program that year. Section Two was now a random selection of students. The fellow professor who had asked

---

[8] Wilkinson, Bruce (2010-07-07). *The Seven Laws of the Learner: How to Teach Almost Anything to Practically Anyone* (p. 80). Multnomah Books. Kindle Edition.

him about his luck in being assigned Section Two hadn't gotten the memo. Bruce recalls, "For the first time, I realized that what I believed about my students made an incredible difference in what they learned in my class."[9]

This raises an important question: what did Jesus expect of his disciples? Did Jesus expect his disciples to grow and change and mature and develop into the world-changing men that they became? Did that expectation affect them?

An equally important question has to do with us and our teaching. What do we expect of our students and does that expectation affect them? Does our expectation of our students predict their growth and maturity?

Captives will be released

It would be great if every section of the gospels began like a Law and Order episode with a date and a time. That way we could see the exact chronology of what is going on. Sometimes it is a bit of a challenge to piece together.

---

[9] Wilkinson, Bruce (2010-07-07). *The Seven Laws of the Learner: How to Teach Almost Anything to Practically Anyone* (p. 82). Multnomah Books. Kindle Edition.

But, it is clear that some time has passed since Jesus' temptation. Luke 4.14b (NLT) records, "Reports about him spread quickly through the whole region." Clearly some time had passed for Jesus to do some miracles and for the word to spread.

Still, early in his ministry, Jesus comes home to Nazareth. As was his custom, he went to the synagogue on the Sabbath. (If anyone ever asks if it is a good idea to go to church out of habit, this is a good verse to point them to.) They ask him to read. Jesus reads a section from Isaiah. It reads like a purpose statement. When he is finished, he rolls up the scroll, hands it to attendant and sits down. All eyes are on him. He says, "The Scripture you've just heard has been fulfilled this very day!" Lk 4:21 NLT. Jesus is saying, "This is what I am about; this is what I came to do." And what had he read in Isaiah?

> "The Spirit of the LORD is upon me,
> for he has anointed me to bring Good News to the poor.
> He has sent me
> to proclaim that captives will be released,
> that the blind will see,
> that the oppressed will be set free,
> and that the time of the LORD's favor has come."
> Luke 4:18–19 (NLT)

Notice the sense of expectation in these verses: the captives will be released; the blind will see; the oppressed will be set free. This suggests from the outset that Jesus expected his teaching to produce results.

Come, follow me

This passage, also early in Jesus' ministry, sheds light on Jesus' expectations. He could have said what he said here in one of at least three ways. There are two ways to ask a question in Greek. One expects a negative answer and the other expects a positive answer. Then there is a command. Jesus language here is somewhere between a question expecting a positive answer and a command. It is not exactly a command, but, as Lenski puts it, "it has the force of an imperative."[10]

English translations universally treat this as an imperative, as you see here: "Jesus called out to them, 'Come, follow me, and I will show you how to fish for people!'" Matthew 4:19 (NLT)

---

[10] *Lenski New Testament Commentary - The Interpretation of St. Matthew's Gospel.*

The question is: what kind of response did Jesus expect? He could have said, "You guys don't want to follow me, do you?" He didn't say it that way. He could have said, "Would you like to follow me?" He didn't say it that way either. The way he did say it has the force of a command that he expected them to follow: "Come, follow me."

The first word in the ESV captures what happened next: "Immediately they left their nets and followed him." Jesus expected the disciples to follow and they did.

Great things will you do

Imagine Jesus sitting around in a circle with his small group. One of Jesus' primary ministries was that of small group leader. He often left the masses to teach his small group of disciples. Much of his teaching was done sitting around in a circle where his small group could ask him questions. This is the context of Jesus' teaching in John 14.

In verse 5 Thomas asks Jesus a question: "Lord, we don't know where you are going, so how can we know the way?" Jesus answers him. I imagine he looked at him as he answered. It is the normal thing to do to look at people when you talk to them. Hold that thought.

In verse 8 Philip made a request of Jesus: "Lord, show us the Father and that will be enough for us." Jesus responded to his request by saying, "Anyone who has seen me has seen the Father." Again, I would guess Jesus looked at Philip as he said this. Imagine you are Philip. Imagine Jesus is looking at you as he teaches. Imagine he is still looking at you in the same paragraph when Jesus says (verse 12), "I tell you the truth, anyone who has faith in me will do what I have been doing. He will do even greater things than these, because I am going to the Father."

Imagine what it felt like for Philip to be sitting in a circle when Jesus said this to him. Jesus says the word, "anyone who has faith. . ." Imagine his eyes are locked on yours when he says it.

What does this mean, by the way, that believers of Christ will do greater things than Jesus did? I remember this verse tripping me up when I first read it. But, look at it from the perspective of history. On the day of Pentecost there were more followers of Christ than Jesus had seen in his lifetime. In twenty years Christianity would have spread through much of the Roman world.

Today, roughly a third—2 billion people on planet earth call themselves Christians. Christianity is the world's largest religion. Consider these words from the Holman Bible Commentary:[11]

> *This is one of the most interesting verses in the Bible. Interpreters have pondered what Jesus meant by telling his disciples that they would do greater things than he, the Son of God, had done. But perhaps the best way to understand the verse is to take it literally, exactly as Jesus said it. Jesus' earthly ministry was limited in time and space. He served the Father for three and one-half years and never outside the boundaries of Palestine. The disciples, on the other hand, as Acts clearly attests, carried out ministry that was greater geographically, in terms of numbers of people reached and long-lasting effect.*

Because this is a shocking verse, we tend to think about how to interpret it. I want you to think about what it felt like for the disciples, sitting around in a circle, as Jesus said these words.

I think they felt believed in.

---

[11] Gangel, K. O. (2000). *Vol. 4: John. Holman New Testament Commentary; Holman Reference (266–267)*. Nashville, TN: Broadman & Holman Publishers.

The gates of hell will not prevail

Imagine how Peter felt when Jesus made this famous statement to him:

> *"Jesus replied, "You are blessed, Simon son of John,*
> *because my Father in heaven has revealed this to you.*
> *You did not learn this from any human being. Now*
> *I say to you that you are Peter (which means 'rock'),*
> *and upon this rock I will build my church, and all the*
> *powers of hell will not conquer it. And I will give you the*
> *keys of the Kingdom of Heaven. Whatever you forbid*
> *on earth will be forbidden in heaven, and whatever*
> *you permit on earth will be permitted in heaven."*
> *Matthew 16:17-19 (NLT)*

Don't worry with interpreting this verse. Don't think about whether the rock refers to Peter himself or Peter's faith. People will be pondering those issues until Christ returns. Just imagine what it felt like for Peter to hear these words. How do you imagine Peter felt?

I think he felt believed in.

Go, make disciples of all nations

It is always a good idea to look at what words meant to their original audience before we try to figure out what they mean to us. There is no greater example of this than with the Great Commission.

Imagine what it felt like for Jesus' disciples to hear these words for the first time:

> *Jesus came and told his disciples, "I have been given all authority in heaven and on earth. Therefore, go and make disciples of all the nations, baptizing them in the name of the Father and the Son and the Holy Spirit. Teach these new disciples to obey all the commands I have given you. And be sure of this: I am with you always, even to the end of the age." Matthew 28:18-20 (NLT)*

Remember it was a much bigger world then. You can get to anyplace on planet earth within 24 hours today—even with a few long connections thrown in. We can Skype people instantly anywhere in the world. It is a much smaller world today.

If they were going to make disciples of all nations, they were going to have to walk. And there were only eleven of them.

If we think of Jesus commissioning his disciples today, we might be tempted to think, "We can do this; this is within our grasp if we work at it." We have lots of talented leaders. We have tons of money. We have technology. We have research on how to grow a church and do evangelism and make disciples. If we think of it globally today, we can imagine making disciples of all nations. How did the original eleven feel as they heard these words?

I think they felt believed in.

Afraid? Probably. Intimidated? Sure. Overwhelmed? You bet!

But, beneath all that fear and intimidation, they had to feel like, "This Jesus who was just raised from the dead believes in us enough to ask us to make disciples of the whole planet." Wow.

What about you?

Do you believe in the people you lead? Do you expect them to change? Do you assume that they will become world-changing disciples? Do you imagine your group will grow and reach people and develop leaders and become a part of the world-wide movement of God?

Or do you imagine it is going to be us four, no more, same as before? Do you imagine we are going to need to just hunker down and huddle together and wait for Jesus to rescue us from this mess?

What do you expect God to do in the lives of your group?

They can feel it. They know it. They know what you expect. Maybe not consciously, but they know it. And very rarely will a student exceed the expectations of his teacher. Children rarely exceed the expectation of their parents. Athletes rarely outperform the expectation of their coaches.

Jesus taught it will be done for us according to our faith. If we believe great things in our students we will see great things in our students.

I'd like to paraphrase the words of William Carey who said, "Expect great things from God; attempt great things for God." Here is the paraphrase: Expect great things from your group; attempt great things with your group. Joe Aldrich said, "What we anticipate in life is usually what we get."[12]

---

[12] Aldrich, Joe Dr (2011-07-20). *Lifestyle Evangelism: Learning to Open Your Life to Those Around You* (p. 176). Multnomah Books. Kindle Edition.

God always works through people. Can you think of a great movement of God that did not involve people? God always works through people.

God always works through people of faith. Faith is the conduit through which His power flows. When we believe that God can do great things through the people we serve, we open the faucet of God's blessings.

Teach like Jesus. Believe in the people you teach. Expect great things from them.

I believe in you

One more thing. Let me say I believe in you. I believe God can use people like you to turn the world upside down. I believe God can use you and your teaching to change lives. I believe a group like yours can double every two years or less. A group of ten that doubles every two years or less can reach 1000 people in ten years. I believe you can do it.

Ask lots of questions

Question and answer is one of the most proven forms of teaching. Its formal adoption dates back at least to the Greek thinkers: Plato, Aristotle and Socrates. Thus the name: Socratic Method.

Jesus asked lots of questions when he taught. In fact, in doing some research, I found this list of 100 questions that Jesus asked. Stan Guthrie has counted nearly 300 questions that Jesus asked. Here are 100 examples:[13]

1. And if you greet your brethren only, what is unusual about that? Do not the unbelievers do the same? (Matt 5:47)
2. Can any of you by worrying add a single moment to your lifespan? Matt 6:27
3. Why are you anxious about clothes? Matt 6:28
4. Why do you notice the splinter in your brother's eye yet fail to perceive the wooden beam in your own eye? (Matt 7:2)

---

[13] http://blog.adw.org/2010/03/answer-the-question-one-hundred-questions-that-jesus-asked/

5. Do people pick grapes from thorn bushes or figs from thistles? (Matt 7:16)
6. Why are you terrified? (Matt 8:26)
7. Why do you harbor evil thoughts? (Matt 9:4)
8. Can the wedding guests mourn so long as the Bridegroom is with them? (Matt 9:15)
9. Do you believe I can do this? (Matt 9:28)
10. What did you go out to the desert to see? (Matt 11:8)
11. To what shall I compare this generation? (Matt 11:6)
12. Which of you who has a sheep that falls into a pit on the Sabbath will not take hold of it and lift it out? (Matt 12:11)
13. How can anyone enter a strong man's house and take hold of his possessions unless he first ties up the strong man? (Matt 12:29)
14. You brood of vipers! How can you say good things when you are evil? (Matt 12:34)
15. Who is my mother? Who are my brothers? (Matt 12:48)
16. Why did you doubt? (Matt 14:31)
17. And why do you break the commandments of God for the sake of your tradition? (Matt 15:3)
18. How many loaves do you have? (Matt 15:34)
19. Do you not yet understand? (Matt 16:8)
20. Who do people say the Son of Man is? (Matt 16:13)
21. But who do you say that I am? (Matt 16:15)
22. What profit would there be for one to gain the whole world and forfeit his life, and

what can one give in exchange for his life? (Matt 16:26)

23. Faithless and perverse generation, how long must I endure you? (Matt 17:17)

24. Why do you ask me about what is good? (Matt 19:16)

25. Can you drink the cup that I am going to drink? (Matt 20:22)

26. What do you want me to do for you? (Matt 20:32)

27. Did you never read the scriptures? (Matt 21:42)

28. Why are you testing me? (Matt 22:18)

29. Blind fools, which is greater, the gold or the temple that makes the gold sacred.... the gift or the altar that makes the gift sacred? (Matt 23:17-19)

30. How are you to avoid being sentenced to hell? (Matt 23:33)

31. Why do you make trouble for the woman? (Matt 26:10)

32. Could you not watch for me one brief hour? (Matt 26:40)

33. Do you think I cannot call upon my Father and he will not provide me at this moment with more than 12 legions of angels? (Matt 26:53)

34. Have you come out as against a robber with swords and clubs to seize me? (Matt 26:53)

35. My God, My God, Why have you forsaken me? (Matt 27:46)

36. Why are you thinking such things in your heart? (Mark 2:8)

37. Is a lamp brought to be put under a basket or under a bed rather than on a lamp stand? (Mark 4:21)
38. Who has touched my clothes? (Mark 5:30)
39. Why this commotion and weeping? (Mark 5:39)
40. Are even you likewise without understanding? (Mark 7:18)
41. Why does this generation seek a sign? (Mark 8:12)
42. Do you not yet understand or comprehend? Are your hearts hardened? Do you have eyes and still not see? Ears and not hear? (Mark 8:17-18)
43. How many wicker baskets full of leftover fragments did you pick up? (Mark 8:19)
44. [To the Blind man] Do you see anything? (Mark 8:23)
45. What were you arguing about on the way? (Mark 9:33)
46. Salt is good, but what if salt becomes flat? (Mark 9:50)
47. What did Moses command you? (Mark 10:3)
48. Do you see these great buildings? They will all be thrown down. (Mark 13:2)
49. Simon, are you asleep? (Mark 14:37)
50. Why were you looking for me? (Luke 2:49)
51. What are you thinking in your hearts? (Luke 5:22)
52. Why do you call me 'Lord, Lord,' and not do what I command? (Luke 6:46)
53. Where is your faith? (Luke 8:25)
54. What is your name? (Luke 8:30)
55. Who touched me? (Luke 8:45)

56. Will you be exalted to heaven? (Luke 10:15)
57. What is written in the law? How do you read it? (Luke 10:26)
58. Which of these three in your opinion was neighbor to the robber's victim? (Luke 10:36)
59. Did not the maker of the outside also make the inside? (Luke 11:40)
60. Friend, who appointed me as your judge and arbiter? (Luke 12:14)
61. If even the smallest things are beyond your control, why are you anxious about the rest? (Luke 12:26)
62. Why do you not judge for yourself what is right? (Luke 12:57)
63. What king, marching into battle, would not first sit down and decide whether with ten thousand troops he can successfully oppose another king marching upon him with twenty thousand troops? (Luke 14:31)
64. If, therefore, you are not trustworthy with worldly wealth, who will trust you with true wealth? (Luke 16:11)
65. Has none but this foreigner returned to give thanks to God? (Luke 17:18)
66. Will not God then secure the rights of his chosen ones who call out to him day and night? (Luke 18:7)
67. But when the Son of Man comes, will he find any faith on earth? (Luke 18:8)
68. For who is greater, the one seated a table or the one who serves? (Luke 22:27)
69. Why are you sleeping? (Luke 22:46)

70. For if those things are done when the wood is green, what will happen when it is dry? (Luke 23:31)
71. What are you discussing as you walk along? (Luke 24:17)
72. Was it not necessary that the Messiah should suffer these things and then enter his glory? (Luke 24:26)
73. Have you anything here to eat? (Luke 24:41)
74. What are you looking for? (John 1:38)
75. How does this concern of yours affect me? (John 2:4)
76. You are a teacher in Israel, and you do not understand this? (John 3: 10)
77. If I tell you about earthly things and you will not believe, how will you believe when I tell you of heavenly things? (John 3: 12)
78. Do you want to be well? (John 5:6)
79. How is it that you seek praise from one another and not seek the praise that comes from God? (John 5:44)
80. If you do not believe Moses' writings, how will you believe me? (John 5:47)
81. Where can we buy enough food for them to eat? (John 6:5)
82. Does this (teaching of the Eucharist) shock you? (John 6:61)
83. Do you also want to leave me? (John 6:67)
84. Why are you trying to kill me? (John 7:19)
85. Woman, where are they, has no one condemned you? (John 8:10)
86. Why do you not understand what I am saying? (John 8:43)

87. Can any of you charge me with sin? (John 8:46)
88. If I am telling you the truth, why do you not believe me? (John 8:46)
89. Are there not twelve hours in a day? (John 11:9)
90. Do you believe this? (John 11:26)
91. Do you realize what I have done for you? (John 13:12)
92. Have I been with you for so long and still you do not know me? (John 14:9)
93. Whom are you looking for? (John 18:4)
94. Shall I not drink the cup the Father gave me? (John 18:11)
95. If I have spoken rightly, why did you strike me? (John 18:23)
96. Do you say [what you say about me] on your own, or have others been telling you about me? (John 18:34)
97. Have you come to believe because you have seen me? (John 20:29)
98. Do you love me? (John 21:16)
99. What if I want John to remain until I come? (John 21:22)
100. What concern is it of yours? (John 21:22)

Where can we get something to eat?

The story of the feeding of the five thousand provides some rich insight into the teaching style of Jesus. It is one of the few times Jesus tells us why he does what he does:

When Jesus looked up and saw a great crowd coming toward him, he said to Philip, "Where shall we buy bread for these people to eat?" He asked this only to test him, for he already had in mind what he was going to do. John 6:5-6 (NIV)

We don't really know why Jesus singled out Philip. Some say it is because he was from Bethsaida, which is in the area. Others argue this is the wrong Bethsaida. What we do know is that it is a good idea to single out a student from time to time. It is a good idea to call upon one student and ask them a question directly. Jesus did it. Teach like Jesus.

I have done a number of training meetings with Dr. Elmer Towns. He does this even when speaking to large crowds. He walks among them. He interacts with them. He asks them questions. He points to individuals and asked them questions. It sure keeps you on your toes. The thought occurs to you, "He might call on me next; I better pay attention." Perhaps this is why Jesus called on Philip.

We don't know why Jesus asked the question of Philip. We do know why he asked the question. He wanted to test Philip. Truth be told, I will bet all the disciples felt tested.

What would the grading of this test look like?
Here is how I would grade it:

A	Jesus, you are the bread of life!
B	"Do whatever he tells you." This is what Jesus' mother said to him at his first miracle. Jesus literally said, "What to me and to you, woman?" I am told it is not actually as rude in Greek as it sounds in English, which is why translators take some liberty with the text. But it wasn't all that sweet of a thing to say, either. I doubt Hallmark was making cards the next year with this slogan. Mary takes the rebuke and just says, "Do whatever he tells you." Not bad advice of any of us.
C	Let's form a study committee. This is what they would have said if they were Baptist. I heard of a church once that was forming a Feasibility Committee to decide whether forming a Study Committee was worth considering.
D	"Send the people away." This isn't recorded in John, but it is in Matthew and Mark. The idea was: make the problem go away. I give them a D, because at least they thought about it and cared.

F	Situation is hopeless. Even Joel Osteen would be depressed.

How did Philip answer? "Eight months' wages would not buy enough bread for each one to have a bite." I give him a D. Not quite as bad as, "Situation is hopeless," but close.

Andrew stepped up and said we have found two fish and five small pieces of bread. Then he adds, "But how far will that go among so many?"

What kind of grade did you give him?

I give him a B-.

By asking the question, Jesus was leading his disciples to the point where they would embrace his teaching, "I am the bread of life." They were not there yet; he still had some work to do.

Who do they say that I am?

One of the classic examples of Jesus using a question to teach is found in Luke 9.18 where Jesus says, "Who do the crowds say that I am?"

Why did Jesus ask this? Did he not know? That could be. When he became human, he set aside some of his god-ness. In another context, he said he did not know the day or the hour when he would return. I think it is more likely, however, that it was a teaching moment for the disciples.

This is what I call a warm up question. It is a get-em talking question. I write small group curriculum for a living. I start nearly every lesson with this kind of question. It is a question to get the group started talking.

People have said to me, "I have tried using discussion questions and my group doesn't want to talk." Do what Jesus did. Get them talking about somebody else. People love to talk about someone else. I think this is why Jesus asked them about what other people thought. It is always easier to talk about what other people think than to share our own convictions or feelings.

Once Jesus got them talking, Jesus narrowed the focus: "Who do you say that I am?"

Peter declared one of the most profound statements in the entire Bible: "You are the Christ, the Son of the living God!"

Stated a different way, Jesus led the disciples to hear one of the most profound statements in the entire Bible. Jesus is the Christ, the Son of the living God.

Question: why did Jesus craft this centrally important teaching in the form of a question? Why not just say it to his disciples: "I am the Christ, the son of the living God!" It would have been a lot safer that way.

A lot of teachers don't like questions because they are into safe and they know that questions are not safe. You ask a question and you have no idea what kind of answer you might get. If you make a statement, you can carefully craft it so you know exactly what you are going to say.

On this occasion of teaching one of the most centrally important things in all the Bible, Jesus chose to use the teaching method of a question.

Why?

Jesus knew when Peter declared him to be "the Christ of God," that Peter would be changed by this declaration.

Jesus taught that we are changed as much by what we say as what we hear. Mark 7:15 (NIV) "Nothing outside a man can make him 'unclean' by going into him. Rather, it is what comes out of a man that makes him 'unclean.'" "What comes out of a man"—what a man speaks is what makes him clean. We are changed by the truth when we speak the truth. When Peter declared Jesus to be the Christ, he believed ever more firmly that Jesus was the Christ.

This is why the Bible makes a big deal about "if you confess with your mouth." (Romans 10.9) It is not that God needs to hear. It is not even that others need to hear. It is that you need to say. When you confess the truth with your mouth, you are changed by that truth.

Jesus' brother, James, spoke about that. He said the tongue (what you say) is like the rudder of your life. Compared to the ship, the rudder is small, but it turns the whole ship. A bit in the mouth of a horse is small compared to the horse. But it can turn the whole horse. A match is small compared to a forest. But a well-placed match can set tho wholo forest on fire. Well placed words can set a whole church on fire. The words you use set the direction of your life.

I think if James were writing today, he wouldn't talk about bits and rudders; he would talk about steering wheels. Your mouth is the steering wheel. You can steer your whole life with your words. Maybe he would talk about a computer. Your mouth is like the keyboard and mouse on your computer. You control the computer and tell it what to do through the mouse and keyboard. So, you control your life by controlling the words.

James had just warned that not many should be teachers. Perhaps he had teachers on his mind when he spoke of the idea that the tongue controls the life. Perhaps he was hinting to the teachers that if you can get people to say the truth, they will be changed by the truth they confess. We are changed more by what we say than what we hear.

A central issue in my theology is the idea that God is a rewarder. (Hebrews 11:6) We must come to Him for reward. We must believe He is a rewarder and we will be rewarded if we come to Him. It is always in our best interest to live the Christian life. It is always good for us to follow God. It is one thing to say these things to the people I lead. It is quite another to lead them through question and answer to say, "I want to follow God because it is good for me to follow God." That is my goal in teaching—to lead people to speak that truth.

If you would like access to question-based Bible studies, see https://www.mybiblestudylessons.com/

Confront

Charles Wesley penned the words, "Gentle Jesus, meek and mild," but that certainly didn't always characterized the way Jesus taught. Sometimes he yelled. Sometimes he got mad and raised his voice. Sometimes he turned over tables.

Confrontational teaching and preaching is out of style. Today, we like a conversational tone. I get that. During my college and seminary years, when I was developing my thoughts on what church ought to be like, I heard way too many of the scream-and-holler-and-spit-and-shout kind of sermons. I got really turned off to this kind of thing. It seemed so angry. It seemed so mean. It seemed so condemning. It didn't seem like Jesus.

Apparently, I was not alone. About this time there began to spring up a whole new generation of kinder, gentler teachers. Voices of people like Max Lucado and Andy Stanley and John Ortberg sounded a softer, gentler tone. I liked that tone.

But, as I study the teaching style of Jesus, it is hard to miss the fact that Jesus was, at least some of the time, very confrontational. Consider these excerpts:

- "Woe to you, teachers of the law and Pharisees, you hypocrites! You shut the kingdom of heaven in men's faces. You yourselves do not enter, nor will you let those enter who are trying to.
- "Woe to you, teachers of the law and Pharisees, you hypocrites! You travel over land and sea to win a single convert, and when he becomes one, you make him twice as much a son of hell as you are.
- "Woe to you, blind guides! You say, 'If anyone swears by the temple, it means nothing; but if anyone swears by the gold of the temple, he is bound by his oath.' You blind fools! Which is greater: the gold, or the temple that makes the gold sacred? You also say, 'If anyone swears by the altar, it means nothing; but if anyone swears by the gift on it, he is bound by his oath.' You blind men! Which is greater: the gift, or the altar that makes the gift sacred? Therefore, he who swears by the altar swears by it and by everything on it. And he who swears by the temple swears by it and by the one who dwells in it. And he who swears by heaven swears by God's throne and by the one who sits on it.
- "Woe to you, teachers of the law and Pharisees, you hypocrites! You give a tenth of your spices--mint, dill and cumin. But you have neglected the more important mat-

ters of the law--justice, mercy and faithful-
ness. You should have practiced the latter,
without neglecting the former. You blind
guides! You strain out a gnat but swallow a
camel.

- "Woe to you, teachers of the law and Pharisees, you hypocrites! You clean the outside of the cup and dish, but inside they
are full of greed and self-indulgence. Blind
Pharisee! First clean the inside of the cup
and dish, and then the outside also will be
clean.

- "Woe to you, teachers of the law and Pharisees, you hypocrites! You are like whitewashed tombs, which look beautiful on the
outside but on the inside are full of dead
men's bones and everything unclean. In
the same way, on the outside you appear
to people as righteous but on the inside
you are full of hypocrisy and wickedness.

- "Woe to you, teachers of the law and Pharisees, you hypocrites! You build tombs for
the prophets and decorate the graves of
the righteous. And you say, 'If we had lived
in the days of our forefathers, we would
not have taken part with them in shed-
ding the blood of the prophets.' So you
testify against yourselves that you are the
descendants of those who murdered the
prophets. Fill up, then, the measure of the
sin of your forefathers!

- "You snakes! You brood of vipers! How will
you escape being condemned to hell?
Therefore I am sending you prophets and
wise men and teachers. Some of them you

will kill and crucify; others you will flog in your synagogues and pursue from town to town. And so upon you will come all the righteous blood that has been shed on earth, from the blood of righteous Abel to the blood of Zechariah son of Berekiah, whom you murdered between the temple and the altar. I tell you the truth, all this will come upon this generation. Matthew 23:13-36 (NIV)

This is, of course, not the only way Jesus taught. But, he didn't shrink back from getting in people's faces: you are sinning and you need to quit.

Do you ever harshly confront sin when you teach? Teach like Jesus.

I had someone complain about my teaching one time that I am too hard on sin. Interesting. I doubt they ever said that about Jesus.

Confrontation is carried on the bridge of relationship. The stronger the relationship, the more harsh can be the rebuke. Growing in Christ is, in part, about growing close to one another so that we can speak honestly into each other's lives.

Jesus rebukes his friends

Jesus harshly rebuked the Pharisees, and they were not the only people he rebuked. Consider this passage. Notice Peter's reaction to Jesus' words:

> *When they had finished breakfast, Jesus said to Simon Peter, "Simon, son of John, do you love me more than these?" He said to him, "Yes, Lord; you know that I love you." He said to him, "Feed my lambs." He said to him a second time, "Simon, son of John, do you love me?" He said to him, "Yes, Lord; you know that I love you." He said to him, "Tend my sheep." He said to him the third time, "Simon, son of John, do you love me?" Peter was grieved because he said to him the third time, "Do you love me?" and he said to him, "Lord, you know everything; you know that I love you." Jesus said to him, "Feed my sheep. John 21:15–17 (ESV)*

Peter was grieved. I think Jesus knew that what he said was going to grieve Peter. I don't think it delighted Jesus to upset Peter. But he knew it was necessary for Peter's own development.

In Matthew 26.33 Peter suggested that he loved Jesus more than the other disciples. "Peter answered him, 'Though they all fall away because of you, I will never fall away.'" You can almost see Peter pounding his enlarged chest and bragging that he loved Jesus the most and he would never be disloyal to Christ.

We know better. We know the story of Peter's denial and the cock crowing and all that. Jesus knew it too. He took special note of Peter and made sure that he was told of the resurrection. "But go, tell his disciples **and Peter** that he is going before you to Galilee. There you will see him, just as he told you." Mark 16:7 (ESV emphasis added.)

By the way, this passage is also an example of the principle we just looked at: Ask questions. Jesus knew that the best way to deal with the issue was not simply confront directly and say, "OK, Peter, you said you loved me more than the rest. You can see now that you don't. You are a prideful person, Peter. Repent." By asking, probing, asking, and asking again, Jesus caused Peter to see his own sin. Only people who see their sin can receive grace.

Peter's denial was a thing that hung in the room. Peter was, of course, elated by Jesus' resurrection. But his joy was tainted by his own failure. Jesus lovingly, yet firmly brings it up. He knew doing so would hurt Peter, but he knew it must be done.

Sometimes there are issues that lie below the surface. They don't come up in day-to-day conversation, but they are there. They are like a sliver of wood that gets lodged just below the surface of the skin, causing considerable pain. It is painful to dig the thing out. It causes more pain, over the long run, to let it sit there.

If you want to teach like Jesus, sometimes you need to confront. Sometimes you need to deal with an issue. Sometimes you need to bring it up.

It ought to grieve you to do so. It ought to break your heart. It should bring you no pleasure. In fact, if it brings you pleasure to bring up another's fault, don't do it. Your heart is still too dark to be used in the hand of God. Deal with your own heart first. It should be sincerely true of what is true of every parent that disciplines: this is going to hurt me more than it hurts you.

Before we rebuke we need to take one step that Jesus did not need to take. He told us to take this step, although he himself did not do so. He didn't need to. "Why do you see the speck that is in your brother's eye, but do not notice the log that is in your own eye?" Matthew 7:3 (ESV) After our own sins are dealt with, we can go with a broken heart.

But, go we must. If you want to teach like Jesus, it is not all feel-good stuff. Sometimes you must deal with the hard stuff. Sometimes you must confront. Sometimes you must say words that hurt.

Words that hurt will heal in the long run. Feel-good words will not. This is the problem with some feel-good preaching you hear today. It is not like Jesus. Jesus' preaching did not always make people feel good. It was redemptive in the long run, but often painful in the short run.

Teach like Jesus.

Jesus rebuked his enemies

Jesus reserved his most scathing rebuke for the most respected people of society: the scribes and the Pharisees.

It is difficult for us to recreate in our mind the scene as it was played out. We look at it from our vantage point. Pharisee has come to mean hypocrite. For church people, Pharisee means, "bad guy." But when Jesus called the Pharisees hypocrites, it was an eye-popping moment. Let's go back in time. Where did the Pharisees come from?

We don't find Pharisees in the Old Testament. Their history is shrouded in mystery. The earliest reference to the Pharisees is around 150 B.C. The story of their origin is a little fuzzy, but here is what we do know.

Alexander the Great conquered the region 330 years before Christ. Alexander loved the Greek way of life. He sought to conquer militarily, but, more importantly, culturally. He spread the Greek language (which explains why the New Testament is written in Greek). He built roads, and spread all things Greek to the region.

A movement developed in Israel to counter this Greek influence. They were known as the Hasideans. The name comes from a Greek transliteration of the Hebrew word for pious or devout. These were the ones who stood against what we might think of as secularism today. They stood against this creeping slide into Greek culture. They called Israel back to their roots.

Most people think that both the Pharisees and the Essenes came out of this movement. The name Pharisee means "separate ones." They separated themselves from the Greek way of life and called Israel to holiness.

The Pharisees were the good guys. They were the respected ones. They were Billy Graham and Mother Teresa. People looked up to them, admired them, and revered them. We think of them as old-fashioned, religious fuddy-duddies. "They were the progressives of the day, willing to adopt new ideas and adapt the law to new situations."[14]

It is hard for us to imagine the shock that came over the faces of the people when Jesus flatly declared, "For I tell you, unless your righteousness exceeds that of the scribes and Pharisees, you will never enter the kingdom of heaven." Matthew 5:20 (ESV)

We hear that and pump our fists and say, "Yeah, get 'em Jesus! Put it to those hypocritical do-gooders who think they are all that!"

When they heard these words, they dropped their heads and thought, "What hope is there for me?"

In this context we look at Matthew 23. The NIV has the caption: Seven Woes. Woe is an old word that could be translated roughly, "You are in trouble!"

---

[14] Brand, C., Draper, C., England, A., Bond, S., Clendenen, E. R., Butler, T. C., & Latta, B. (2003). *Holman Illustrated Bible Dictionary* (917). Nashville, TN: Holman Bible Publishers.

Let's look at a few of Jesus' accusations against these most respected leaders:

- Child of hell (vs. 15)
- Blind guides (vss. 16, 24)
- Hypocrites (vss. 23, 25, 27, 29)
- Whitewashed tombs (vs. 27)
- Full of dead people's bones (vs. 27)
- Full of hypocrisy and lawlessness (vs. 28)
- Serpents (vs. 33)
- Brood of vipers (vs. 33)

Verse 33 has the crescendo: "You serpents, you brood of vipers, how are you to escape being sentenced to hell?" Matthew 23:33 (ESV)

Do you ever teach like that? Not very fashionable in our day. And, let me be quick to point out, this is not the only approach Jesus used. He was often quite different in his tone—so gentle that children felt safe coming to him and parents felt safe bringing their children to him. Parents don't put their babies in the arms of angry men.

Teaching like Jesus is not always the same. It has variety. Sometimes it is harsh and in-your face. Sometimes it is straightforward and matter-of-fact. Sometimes it is inspiring and uplifting. Sometimes it is comforting.

Notice how Jesus closes this harsh reprimand. He reminds me of a good parent who disciplines the child, then holds and hugs and reminds the child that he is loved, "O Jerusalem, Jerusalem, the city that kills the prophets and stones those who are sent to it! How often would I have gathered your children together as a hen gathers her brood under her wings, and you would not!" Matthew 23:37 (ESV)

The NIV has it, "I have longed to gather your children." God's Word: "How often I wanted to gather your people." Barclay calls it a "poignant tragedy of rejected love."[15] Weirsbe says, "It is a picture of love, tender care, and a willingness to die to protect others.[16] God is pictured in the Bible as a jilted lover pining for his beloved.

I heard recently on the news of a terrible tornado that ripped through the East. A mother, wishing to protect her daughter, put her in the bathtub, and then laid on top of her. The house was crushed in the tornado. The mother died; the child lived. The mother would have done it all again.

---

[15] *Barclay's Daily Study Bible (NT).*

[16] *Bible Exposition Commentary (BE Series) - New Testament - The Bible Exposition Commentary – New Testament, Volume 1*

This is the picture Jesus is painting here. The mother hen calls her young. She wishes to gather them under her wings. There is a storm coming. She is willing to die to protect her young.

And Jesus, of course, does die. He dies so we can live. But, we must be willing. The same word is used twice in this verse. Jesus is saying "I was willing; you were not willing."

We are getting a little off topic here. This chapter is about the idea that Jesus was sometimes quite harsh in his teaching. Here is the point I am getting at here: Jesus was both harsh and tender.

You don't get the idea that Jesus enjoyed being harsh. I have heard some preachers preach that way—as if they enjoyed giving the scolding. That is not teaching like Jesus. If we would teach like Jesus we must sometimes scold and do so harshly, but always with a broken heart. Always wishing we didn't have to say these things. Always hoping the sinner will repent. Always ready to receive them when they do.

Teach like Jesus.

Hands-on

It is clear that many of Jesus' miracles are really acted out parables. A classic example is the calming of the storm. It is not just a story about an historical event. It is a lesson on how Jesus can get us through the storms of life. I love what John Ortberg says about this story: "Peace doesn't come from finding a lake with no storms. It comes from having Jesus in the boat."[17]

Jesus taught a very important lesson that day on the lake. But, he didn't do it with PowerPoint and a good lecture. He did it with a hands-on approach. Jesus acted out the parable by allowing the disciples to get in a storm, and then calming it before their very eyes. His way was unforgettable. Hands-on often is.

Consider the story of Jesus cursing the fruitless tree. Mark 11.13 explains that it was not the season for figs—thus no figs. Jesus curses it anyway. Why? It is an acted out parable. He is teaching what he taught in John 15 that, "He cuts off every

---

[17] John Ortberg, *The Me I Want to Be*, p. 115.

branch that bears no fruit." This way of teaching the lesson was unforgettable.

The ultimate example, of course, was the cross. And it goes without saying that it was more than an acted-out parable. But, what a teaching on being willing to humble yourself and put up with mistreatment and turning the other cheek. Paul taught this lesson through a question, "Why not rather be wronged?" Jesus taught it in an unforgettable way on the cross.

The more senses you can engage, the better. One way to do this is to use movie clips. Here are a few sites that provide short videos you can use in teaching:

- www.sermonspice.com
- www.wingclips.com
- www.bluefishtv.com
- www.ignitermedia.com
- www.youtube.com

Video is one way to spice up your lesson but it is not the only way. Give them something they can touch and feel. Give them something they can taste and smell. The more senses you can engage, the better.

Show me a denarius

In Luke 20 we read that the Pharisees were out to get Jesus. But, because of his popularity with the folks, they were struggling to find a way to do it. So they sent a spy to ask this question, "Is it right for us to pay taxes to Caesar or not?" Luke 20:22 (NIV)

The trap worked like this:

Response	Result
Jesus says it is right to pay taxes.	Jesus makes the people mad. They hated Rome.
Jesus says it is wrong to pay taxes.	Jesus gets in trouble with Rome. The Pharisees now have something they can hang him on.

Jesus, of course, was smarter than their trap. His response was, "Then give back to Caesar what is Caesar's, and to God what is God's." Luke 20:25 (NIV)

What I would like to draw your attention to is the detail of how Jesus responded. "Show me a denarius. Whose image and inscription are on it?" "Caesar's," they replied. Luke 20:24 (NIV)

I picture it like this. Jesus asks for a coin. Someone pulls it out of his pocket and hands it to Jesus. Jesus pauses for dramatic effect as he looks at the coin. Perhaps he flips it up in the air a couple of times. (Good teachers know how to use silence as they teach.) Then he holds it up for all to see. He holds it up and asks the question about whose picture was on it.

Why did he actually ask for a coin? Why did he hold it up? Why didn't he just talk about it? Because Jesus knew that we are impacted as much by what we see as what we hear. I wonder if he passed the coin back to the person who asked the question and let him hold it and look at it himself. Just a guess.

Effective teachers do this. They consistently use stuff that you can touch and feel and hold and smell and taste. The old fashioned term for this is object lesson. All effective teachers use them.

Watch Andy Stanley sometime. Northpoint's production team will have all kinds of props and stuff on the stage. They will redecorate the stage every series to correspond to the messages Andy will preach.

As for what you see here. . .

While Jesus was teaching in the temple he observed two things. He observed a woman who gave two small coins. He taught about that, as we will discuss in another place. Then, he noticed the buildings. He could have introduced this sermon about his second coming in a very abstract way, "Today, I want to talk to you about when I will come back again." He didn't. Jesus was very hands-on. He saw the building made of stones and stated his teaching with that observation:

> *Some of his disciples were remarking about how the temple was adorned with beautiful stones and with gifts dedicated to God. But Jesus said, "As for what you see here, the time will come when not one stone will be left on another; every one of them will be thrown down." Luke 21:5–6 (NIV)*

Lewis taught that we are amphibious beings—one foot in the spirit world and one foot in the physical world. We are both a Spirit that inhabits a body and we are a body that contains a spirit. Good teachers touch both. They speak to the spiritual realm, but they do it through the realm of the physical. Jesus did it all the time.

Teach like Jesus.

Give me a drink

Teaching is about connecting the Bible to life. We either start with the Bible and eventually connect it to life, or we start with life and show how the Bible connects to it. There is some debate as to which is the better approach. The majority report among serious-minded Bible students is that we ought to start with the Bible. This is called expository preaching. We start with the text, we expose (expose is the root meaning of expository) the meaning of the text, and we apply it to life. It is a very Bible-centered approach and, as I said, the favorite among serious-minded Bible students.

The other approach is called topical preaching or felt-need preaching. In this approach, we start with life and ask what the Bible has to say about it. Sermon titles often sound like the cover article of a Reader's Digest. Examples would be things like:

- How to win over worry
- Three steps to getting control of your finances
- How to raise happy, healthy kids
- Finding hope when life looks hopeless

Serious-minded students tend to think of these kinds of sermons as light and fluffy and not as biblical as expository sermons. Rick Warren is the quintessential topical preacher. He describes his preaching by saying:[18]

> Each week I begin with a need, hurt, or interest and then move to what God has to say about it in his Word. Rather than concentrating on a single passage, I will use many verses from many passages that speak to the topic. I call this type of preaching "verse-with-verse" exposition, or topical exposition.

Although Rick is extremely popular with the unchurched, his approach is not so well-liked

---

[18] Warren, Rick (2004). *The Purpose Driven- Church: Growth Without Compromising Your Message and Mission* (Kindle Locations 3649-3652). Zondervan. Kindle Edition.

within tho preaching community. He has gotten plenty of criticism for his approach. He says: [19]

> Today, "preaching to felt needs" is scorned and criticized in some circles as a cheapening of the Gospel and a sellout to consumerism. I want to state this in the clearest way possible: Beginning a message with people's felt needs is more than a marketing tool! It is based on the theological fact that God chooses to reveal himself to man according to our needs! Both the Old and New Testaments are filled with examples of this.

Here is my question: what kind of preaching did Jesus do? If we would teach like Jesus, would we lean toward expository preaching or topical preaching? By the way, although Rick Warren is a big fan of topical preaching for seekers, he advises that we do both topical and expository preaching:[20]

> Both verse-by-verse (book) exposition and verse-with-verse (topical) exposition are necessary in order to grow a healthy church. Book exposition works best for edification. Topical exposition works best for evangelism.

---

[19] Warren, Rick (2004). *The Purpose Driven- Church: Growth Without Compromising Your Message and Mission* (Kindle Locations 3649-3652). Zondervan. Kindle Edition.

[20] Warren, Rick (2004). The Purpose Driven- Church: Growth Without Compromising Your Message and Mission (Kindle Locations 3663-3665). Zondervan. Kindle Edition.

However, the real question is not what does Rick Warren think but what would Jesus do? How did Jesus teach? It seems to me it was exclusively topical. He started where people were. As far as the record shows, Jesus never gave one expository message.

He did stand up in his home town and read from Isaiah and said, "Today this scripture is fulfilled in your hearing." Luke 4:21 (NIV) but I would not call that expository preaching. In the Sermon on the Mount, he said, "You have heard that it was said. . ." But, again, I wouldn't call that expository teaching either. Jesus normally started where people were and talked about how the kingdom life related to their lives.

A classic example of this is the conversation with the woman at the well. He begins the dialogue by asking her for a drink. (This is an example of something we will discuss later: Jesus' teaching was unexpected.) He did the shocking thing. You can tell she was shocked by her response: "The woman was surprised, for Jews refuse to have anything to do with Samaritans. She said to Jesus, 'You are a Jew, and I am a Samaritan woman. Why are you asking me for a drink?'" John 4:9 (NLT)

The point I want to draw out of this teaching in this section, however, does not have to do with how Jesus shocked this woman. Notice how he started where she was. He is going to teach on living water and he starts by asking for a drink. Brilliant.

Other examples

There are numerous examples of Jesus teaching using this hands-on approach. Here are a few:

- Jesus said he was the bread of life. Before doing so, he fed the five thousand bread and fish.
- Jesus taught us that he is with us in the storms. He calmed a real storm to teach this lesson.
- Jesus wanted to teach about the importance of fruitfulness. In John 15 Jesus taught this directly: "He cuts off every branch in me that bears no fruit, while every branch that does bear fruit he prunes so that it will be even more fruitful." John 15:2 (NIV) In Matthew 11 Jesus taught this lesson with a hands-on approach, cursing a tree that did not bear fruit.
- Jesus wanted to teach about his glory. He was transfigured. His clothes glowed in the light. Moses and Elijah showed up. There is a lesson on glory they will never forget.

- Jesus didn't say, "If you have small faith you can do big things." He said, "If you have faith like a grain of mustard seed, you will say to this mountain, 'Move from here to there,' and it will move, and nothing will be impossible for you." Matthew 17:20 (ESV) Do you see the difference? Teach like Jesus.
- Jesus could have said, "Try to avoid temptation altogether. If you can avoid the temptation, you can avoid the sin." Instead, Jesus said, "And if your hand or your foot causes you to sin, cut it off and throw it away. It is better for you to enter life crippled or lame than with two hands or two feet to be thrown into the eternal fire." Matthew 18:8 (ESV) "Cut it off and throw it away." There is a word picture you will not soon forget.
- Jesus was asked, "Who is the greatest in the kingdom of heaven?" Before Jesus answered, he pulled a child in front of them. (This will be more significant when you understand how children were treated back in the day. We will explore that in the chapter on kid-friendly.) With the child in front of them, he said, "Whoever humbles himself like this child is the greatest in the kingdom of heaven. Whoever receives one such child in my name receives me," Matthew 18:4, 5 (ESV). We gloss over this so quickly. Can you imagine a preacher speaking on humility and calling a child to join him on the stage? The whole time he is preaching he is pointing to the child. "Be humble like

this child here." This kind of hands-on approach was commonplace for Jesus.

The world was Jesus' flannel-graph. He constantly painted on the tapestry of the world.

Bill Hybels explains how simple, yet powerful, this can be:[21]

> *I was preparing to teach on the tenderness of God. The idea occurred to me to preach from the passage that says, "A bruised reed God will not allow to break." So I got a bruised reed and held it while I said, "Some of you feel like a bruised reed today." I talked to them about the tenderness of God while holding that simple prop.*
>
> *As I visited the offices or homes of our people over the following weeks, many had a bruised reed on their desk or taped to their refrigerator. It was amazing. People remember that stuff.*

Using all five senses

Effective teachers teach using all five senses. Here are some examples from my favorite author's book, KidTeach. (She has many more in her book.)[22]

---

[21] http://www.churchleaders.com/pastors/pastor-articles/156273-bill-hybels-6-sure-fire-ways-to-improve-your-preaching.html?p=2

[22] *KidTeach*, Missy Hunt, pages 133ff.

Hearing

- Music/Singing
- Clapping, snapping, banging, drumming, or playing instruments
- Reciting memory verses together

Seeing

- Posters
- Maps
- Pictures of Bible characters
- Video clips

Smelling

- Burn scented candles that seem to fit the "theme" of the lesson
- Food (fish, lemons, freshly baked bread)
- Objects from nature (pine needles, wood chips, flowers)
- Perfumes

Taste

- Food that is cold – Think about Jonah on a ship and what he *might have* eaten while rocking and rolling out on the open sea (most likely it was not a nice hot meal – taking a little freedom here to imagine what *might have been*).
- Food that is hot – Think nice, steamy bowl of soup when Esau gives up his birthright for some lentil stew.
- Food that is bland – Think plain, unsalted cracker as manna is eaten by the Israelites.

Touch

- Shaving cream (write or draw in it or make shapes with it)
- Objects from nature
- Objects from home (this can be almost anything). Check out a series of books called "Object Talks" and "Object Lessons" at amazon. com or at your local book store.

Some of the ideas are geared more to kid teachers but many of them can be adapted for adult use. Adults are generally more open to a creative, hands-on approach than we are willing to use such an approach.

Modern science

Modern science has proven beyond doubt that pictures help persuade. Consider this research:[23]

> To ensure they were starting with a clean slate, Gibson and Zillman used a fictitious threat—"Blowing Rock Disease"—which was said to be a newly identified illness spread by ticks in the American Southeast. Children were deemed particularly vulnerable to this new danger.
>
> Gibson and Zillman asked 135 people, mainly university students, to read two articles—the first

---

[23] Gardner, Daniel (2008-07-17). *The Science of Fear: How the Culture of Fear Manipulates Your Brain* (pp. 158-159). Plume. Kindle Edition

78

about wetlands and another about Blowing Rock
Disease—taken from national news magazines, with
questions about facts and opinions asked after each.
The first article really did come from a national news
magazine. The second was fictitious, but made to look
like a typical piece from the magazine U.S. News &
World Report, with a headline that read, "Ticks Cutting
a Mean Path: Areas in the Southeast Hardest Hit by
Deadly New Disease." Participants were presented with
one of several versions of the article. One was text only.
The second also had photos of ticks, seen in creepy
close-up. The third had the ticks plus photos of children
who were said to be infected. The text of the article
was the same in every case—it informed the reader
that children were at more risk than adults, and it had
profiles of children who had contracted the disease.

If factual information and logic were all there were to
risk perception, the estimates of the danger posed by
"Blowing Rock Disease" would have been the same no
matter which version of the article they read. But those
who read the version that had no pictures gave a lower
estimate of the risk than all the others. Those who got
the second version of the story—with photos of ticks—
believed the risk was significantly higher, while those
who saw photos of ticks and children pegged the risk
higher still.

Based on this research and the example of Jesus,
I try to use pictures as often as I can when I teach.
Great thing about the world in which we live, in—
this is easier than ever to do. Do a Google search
for almost anything and you can find a picture.
Just click on the *images* tab and up pops some

pictures that you can use with your teaching. Last week I told a story about a man who wrote to the IRS, "I feel terrible about the fact that I have not paid my taxes. I can't sleep at night. Here is a check for $10,000. P.S. If I still can't sleep at night, I will send you the rest." While I was telling that story, this simple picture was on the screen:

I told this story about anger:[24]

> *A young girl who was writing a paper for school came to her father and asked, "Dad, what is the difference between anger and exasperation?"*
>
> *The father replied, "It is mostly a matter of degree. Let me show you what I mean."*

---

[24] http://www.santabanta.com/jokes.asp?catid=4487

With that the father went to the telephone and dialed a number at random. To the man who answered the phone, he said, "Hello, is Melvin there?"

The man answered, "There is no one living here named Melvin. Why don`t you learn to look up numbers before you dial?"

"See," said the father to his daughter. "That man was not a bit happy with our call. He was probably very busy with something and we annoyed him. Now watch...."

The father dialed the number again. "Hello, is Melvin there?"asked the father.

"Now look here!" came the heated reply. "You just called this number and I told you that there is no Melvin here! You`ve got lot of guts calling again!" The receiver slammed down hard.

The father turned to his daughter and said, "You see, that was anger. Now I`ll show you what exasperation means."

He dialed the same number, and when a violent voice roared, "Hello!"

The father calmly said, "Hello, this is Melvin. Have there been any calls for me?"

The whole time I was telling that story, this picture was on the screen:

The great communicators all do this. They get out stuff that you can touch and feel and see and smell. Bill Hybels talks about how he has seen this work:[25]

> You must also devote time toward creativity. It is so easy for us to fall into ruts and never vary our styles. We urge our teachers at Willow to drop the spoon-fed approach and shake things up once in a while. We encourage them to use a question-asking style or some props instead of just standing at the pulpit with a Bible in hand. We've found props to be remarkably helpful. I was talking about the pressures of life once, and I brought out a chemistry set complete with Bunsen burner. When I lit that Bunsen burner and put a beaker over it and stuff started boiling, people were really listening—all because I used that one little prop.

[25] http://www.churchleaders.com/pastors/pastor-articles/156273-bill-hybels-6-sure-fire-ways-to-improve-your-preaching.html?p=2

Props are cool. But they are not enough. You must love the people you teach and they must know that you love them. That is the topic of the next chapter.

Love Like Jesus

Rarely do we learn from people unless we feel that they love us. If we feel they love us, we can handle their rebuke. We can accept their criticism. We play along when they ask us to do something a little goofy and hands-on. We can accept the word they have for us.

If we don't feel they love us, nothing else matters. We don't want to hear anything they have to say.

There are two issues. The teacher must love the student and the student must perceive he is loved.

Jesus was an effective teacher, in part, because people knew that he loved them. Even outsiders observed Jesus and said, "Behold how he loved." (John 11:36)

If you would teach like Jesus, you must begin by loving like Jesus. As the old saying goes, "People don't care how much you know until they know how much you care."

Eat like Jesus

How do we express love? In the love chapter, Paul speaks of giving everything he has to the poor and giving his body to be burned. Sometimes love calls for that. Jesus knew—sometimes love means paying the ultimate price.

But, Jesus knew something else as well. Sometimes love is pedestrian. It is ordinary. It is earthy. If you want to show your kid you love him, go throw a ball in the back yard with him. Disneyland is nice, but so is a lot of ordinary stuff. If you want to show your wife you love her, sit down on the couch and talk. Or, do the dishes. Or, buy her a $3 card. Love doesn't always mean hiring a marching band.

Consider this example of Jesus: "As Jesus was speaking, one of the Pharisees invited him home for a meal. So he went in and took his place at the table". Luke 11:37 (NLT) Love is spelled T.I.M.E. It means hanging out. It means breaking bread. It means conversation and laughter and questions and showing an interest in the people you would teach.

Teaching is not just what you do when you are in front of a class. Teaching is a way of life. It is not just what you do on Sunday; it is how you live the rest of the week. It is not just presenting to the group; it is presence with the group.

The Navigators call this the "with them" principle, based on Mark 3:14 (NIV) "He appointed twelve—designating them apostles—that they might be **with him** and that he might send them out to preach." [emphasis added]

If you would teach like Jesus, spend time with the people you would teach. Eat with them. Eat like Jesus.

With them in sorrow

Pastors know that if they stay at a church long enough they can lead the church. If they can show up at enough hospital bed sides, people will follow. Once a pastor has done a funeral for family, that family will follow him anywhere.

Of course, the tricky thing with Jesus is that he tended to interrupt the funerals. The funerals Jesus attended didn't end in a burial; they ended in a resurrection.

But on the occasion of the funeral for a friend, Jesus wept before anyone celebrated. He was with them in their time of grief. It is fascinating to consider that Jesus could have easily healed Lazarus from a distance and saved himself from grief. Whatever else was going on with Jesus as he waited two days to see Lazarus he was demonstrating something very important about teaching.

Good teachers know how to grieve with the people they teach.

This point is punctuated in scripture because it is the shortest verse in all the Bible: "Jesus wept." John 11.35.

Back to John 11.35. It is the same in almost any translation. It simply means that Jesus cried. He didn't wail like the others at the funeral did; a different word is used there. He quietly cried. And people saw it and said, "See how he loved him."

People will know that you love them when you are with them in their time of grief. They will listen to anything you have to say if you will be with them in their time of grief.

Times of grief don't always come at convenient times. It sometimes means getting up in the middle of the night to be with a family. It sometimes means a long drive. I had a teacher share at a training meeting one time and he told of taking three trips to Chicago in the last month to be with people in the hospital. He lived in St. Louis. It's a five hour drive. Do you think he ever had an attendance problem with that family?

I had a guy in my class one time with some medical problems that took a while to sort out. His wife was a school teacher and could only take so many days off. He didn't have other family in the area. One day I walked into this hospital room with my laptop. "I am just going to sit here all day and work. If you want to visit, I am happy to. If you want to sleep, go ahead. You don't need to entertain me. I will be here if you need me."

A couple of years later in class we were talking about what it means to be the church. With tears in his eyes he told of the time I didn't just visit; I stayed.

Grief makes us feel uncomfortable so we tend to draw back. We need to move in. Get close in times of grief. You don't have to know what to say. Just be there. Just be there.

Touch like Jesus

Ever notice how often the Bible records that Jesus touched someone? If we restrict our search to the first gospel, here is what we come up with:

- Matthew 8:3 (NIV) Jesus reached out his hand and **touched** the man. "I am willing," he said. "Be clean!" Immediately he was cured of his leprosy.
- Matthew 8:15 (NIV) He **touched** her hand and the fever left her, and she got up and began to wait on him
- Matthew 9:29 (NIV) Then he **touched** their eyes and said, "According to your faith will it be done to you";
- Matthew 17:7 (NIV) But Jesus came and **touched** them. "Get up," he said. "Don't be afraid."
- Matthew 20:34 (NIV) Jesus had compassion on them and **touched** their eyes. Immediately they received their sight and followed him.

Why did Jesus touch so much? He knew we needed it. We thrive on it. He designed us that way.

In the 1940s it was still novel to believe that disease was spread through contact. Rene Spitz conducted an experiment where he took babies whose mothers were in prison and separated them from all physical contact. The babies were fed, clothed, kept warm and clean but were not touched or held. They were not played with or handled. They were not hugged.

Spitz was a believer in the new theory of germs and thought that isolating the babies from human contact and the germs that came with that would serve the babies well. Boy, was he wrong. The babies became withdrawn and sickly. They lost weight. Many died.

In a tragic irony, the babies had all kinds of infections. In one institution, the mortality rate to measles was 40% compared to the average rate of 0.5%. In the cleanest, most sterile environment on the planet, the death rate was above 75%.[26]

People need to be touched. Jesus touched. Touch like Jesus.

Listen

It is curious that the phrase "Jesus listened" never occurs in any of the major translations of the Bible. (Weymouth and Montgomery Translations have the phrase twice and once, respectively.) We do have the phrase, "Jesus asked. . ." 23 times in

---

[26] http://dougduncan.info/2008/12/lack-of-touch-can-kill/

the NIV and the phrases, "Jesus heard" or "hearing this, Jesus. . ." 10 times in the NIV. The Bible doesn't say Jesus listened; it shows that he did.

One of the best examples of Jesus listening is in the story of the road to Emmaus. Read this with a view to observing Jesus as a listener. Look at how long he listens before he jumps in. Eugene Peterson's paraphrase *The Message* is characteristically fresh:

> That same day two of them were walking to the village Emmaus, about seven miles out of Jerusalem. They were deep in conversation, going over all these things that had happened. In the middle of their talk and questions, Jesus came up and walked along with them. But they were not able to recognize who he was.
>
> He asked, "What's this you're discussing so intently as you walk along?"
>
> They just stood there, long-faced, like they had lost their best friend. Then one of them, his name was Cleopas, said, "Are you the only one in Jerusalem who hasn't heard what's happened during the last few days?"
>
> He said, "What has happened?"
>
> They said, "The things that happened to Jesus the Nazarene. He was a man of God, a prophet, dynamic in work and word, blessed by both God and all the

people. Then our high priests and leaders betrayed him, got him sentenced to death, and crucified him. And we had our hopes up that he was the One, the One about to deliver Israel. And it is now the third day since it happened. But now some of our women have completely confused us. Early this morning they were at the tomb and couldn't find his body. They came back with the story that they had seen a vision of angels who said he was alive. Some of our friends went off to the tomb to check and found it empty just as the women said, but they didn't see Jesus."

Then he said to them, "So thick-headed! So slow-hearted! Why can't you simply believe all that the prophets said? Don't you see that these things had to happen, that the Messiah had to suffer and only then enter into his glory?" Then he started at the beginning, with the Books of Moses, and went on through all the Prophets, pointing out everything in the Scriptures that referred to him. Luke 24.13 – 27 Message

Learning to listen well will help you in every arena of life. You will have a better marriage and better relationship with your kids. Your friendships will be better. You will get better reviews at work. Good listeners make better managers, better leaders, and better teachers. They probably make more money.

Listening well has been found to distinguish the best managers, teachers, and leaders. Among those who are in the helping professions, like physicians or social workers, such deep listening numbers among the top three abilities of those whose work has been rated as outstanding by their organizations.[27]

How do you listen well? Here are a few tips:

- Remove distractions. Choose a restaurant that is quiet.
- Notice body language. Non-verbal is more than half of the communication.
- Repeat or paraphrase as needed. If you are not sure you are hearing correctly, say something like, "What I hear you saying is. .."
- Ask follow up questions. Probe. Ask the six reporter's friends: who, what, where, when, why and how.
- Emotional feedback. Say, "It seems you are feeling. .."
- Face the speaker.
- Maintain eye contact without being weird. Too much can creep them out; too little will let them know you are not that interested.
- The magic two seconds. When they finish, make sure they are finished. Wait two seconds to make sure they are finished and not just taking a breath or gathering their thoughts. This is what the Bible means when it speaks of being slow to speak.
- Never interrupt.
- If your mind drifts, ask them to repeat. A lot of advice on listening comes down to this:

---

[27] Goleman, Daniel (2006-09-26). *Social Intelligence: The New Science of Human Relationships* (p. 88). Bantam. Kindle Edition

do it perfectly. Good luck with that. When we don't listen well and our mind is a million miles away, admit it. Say something like, "I am so sorry, can you say that one more time?"

- Ask: is there anything more? Bill Hybels talks about the last ten percent. It is often easy to communicate the first 90%. Good listeners get the 10% that really matters. Keep asking: what else?
- Don't judge. Nothing stops the flow of information like a judgmental attitude.

If you want your people to listen to you, listen to them.

In their space

There is nothing like getting into a person's home to really get to know them. I cannot imagine having a friend I considered to be close unless I had been in their home dozens of times and they had been in mine the same.

You learn so much by getting into people's homes. You learn about their hobbies, how they decorate, who they have pictures of, and what they like to read. Every teacher would do well to get into the home of everyone in his or her group every year.

Jesus said to Zacchaeus, "I am coming to your house today." We ought to say to our people from time to time, "I'd like to come over some time and visit."

Jesus was in people's homes. Teach like Jesus. Love like Jesus.

Of course, this could be overdone. I stopped by to visit a guy once and asked if I could come in and visit. "Uh, I am not much of a house keeper," was his reply. I took this to mean he didn't want me to come in and visit. You will have people that don't want an in-house visit. But, for the rest, here is how to make an annual in-house visit:

- Make an appointment.
- Communicate that you will be doing this with everyone and there is not something wrong with them—particularly if they are not regular attendees.
- Keep it short. There is an exception to this rule, of course, and that is if they want you to stay longer. Don't give them the impression you have to run off. But don't feel obligated to fill two hours when thirty minutes will do.
- Observe their life. Notice the pictures on the wall. Did they have a boat out front? What kind of movies do they watch? What

can you learn about them from seeing their space?

- Ask if you can turn the TV down. Hopefully, they will turn it off.
- Ask about their life. Ask about their kids. Ask about the parents. Ask about the work. Ask about their extended family. Ask about their history—how long they have lived here and what kind of church they went to growing up.
- Ask how you can pray for them.
- Pray together.

Give like Jesus

Small tokens of appreciation can demonstrate you care. Jesus' whole life was about giving. God so loved the world that he gave. We should give too. Give like Jesus.

Remember birthdays and anniversaries

This is easier than it has ever been. Your phone likely has a feature where you can set up a recurring event. Set one up for each person in your group. Call, text, or send a card on their birthday. I am a big believer in making life easy on yourself. Buy a box of birthday cards instead of making 12 trips to the store. I don't think FACEBOOK is all that effective for this. Because everyone can see it is their birthday on

FACEBOOK, sending a birthday greeting there will get lost in the pile.

Serve like Jesus

Sometimes sitting is not enough. Sometimes weeping with them is not enough. Sometimes, we need to do something. Sometimes, we need to serve.

Once again we have an incredible example in the life of Jesus who came not to be served but to serve. He healed. He fed. He helped. He wrapped a towel around his waist and washed feet. Jesus knew: **servants never lack an audience.** If you serve them they will come.

In my experience, this is one area that small groups do pretty well at. So, allow me to model what you ought to do every so often in your teaching. Let me just say: keep up the good work.

Facebook

I mentioned earlier that I don't think Facebook is all that good a way to wish someone happy birthday. On my birthday, I have received hundreds of birthday wishes. I appreciate them, but one more from my teacher probably is not going to mean that much. There are some ways you can express love on Facebook.

Let's reduce it to a Proverb: Get on every member and every prospect's Facebook wall every week. Comment as appropriate. Show an interest in their life.

Say the words: I love you

Jesus didn't leave his feelings for his people up to the imagination. He told them. He said the words: I love you. (John 13.34; John 15.9, 12) Love like Jesus.

Pray like Jesus

Jesus prayed for his people and we should too. A slogan would look like this: Every teacher praying for every member and every prospect every week. You might email your people from time to time and ask them what you can pray for them about. Alternatively, you might email them and mention that you prayed for them this morning.

The relationship of the teacher and the students has as much to do with success in teaching as anything that happens in class. People rarely learn from someone unless they feel like they are loved.

Love like Jesus.

Intriguing

They loved him or they hated him. They wanted to crown him king. They wanted to (and did) crucify him. No one looked at their watches. Jesus' teaching was exciting. It was intriguing. It captured their attention and imagination. They got mad. They loved. They were confused. They argued. Jesus' teaching caused an uproar. Jesus was controversial and never boring. Consider these words:

> When he said these things, the people were again divided in their opinions about him. Some said, "He's demon possessed and out of his mind. Why listen to a man like that?" Others said, "This doesn't sound like a man possessed by a demon! Can a demon open the eyes of the blind?" John 10:19–21 (NIT)

Does this describe the response to your teaching? Does it describe the last Bible Study Group you attended?

"When Aeschines spoke, they said, 'How well he speaks.' But when Demosthenes spoke, they said,

'Let us march against Philip.'"[28] Jesus was more like Demosthenes. People were ready to march.

Consider Matthew 7:28 (NIV): When Jesus had finished saying these things, the crowds were amazed at his teaching.

I draw your attention to the word "amazed." Look how it is translated in various places. (These from the NLT.)[29]

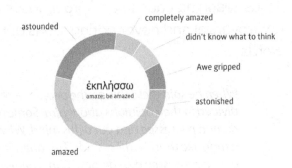

Another way to mine the meaning of a word is to see how this same verse is translated in various translations. I call this vertical and horizontal word study. Here are a few examples [emphasis added].

---

[28] http://en.wikipedia.org/wiki/Demosthenes

[29] Copyright Faithlife Corporation, makers of Logos Bible Software – www.logos.com

- Matthew 7:28 (NIV) 28 When Jesus had finished saying these things, the crowds were **amazed** at his teaching,
- Matthew 7:28 (CEV) 28 When Jesus finished speaking, the crowds were **surprised** at his teaching.
- Matthew 7:28 (ESV) 28 And when Jesus finished these sayings, the crowds were **astonished** at his teaching,
- Matthew 7:28 (MSG) 28 When Jesus concluded his address, the crowd **burst into applause**. They had never heard teaching like this.
- Matthew 7:28 (AMP) 28 When Jesus had finished these sayings [the Sermon on the Mount], the crowds were **astonished and overwhelmed with bewildered wonder** at His teaching,

The Greek word is formed by combining two Greek words. Taken together, it could be translated, "To stand out" or "outstanding." It sounds like the word ecstasy.

Do you get something of the flavor of this word that described Jesus' teaching? Does it describe the last Bible Study you went to? Does it describe the last Bible Study you taught? Does it make you want to pray this prayer: "Lord, help me be more like Jesus."?

Repeat these statements (Say them out loud if you are in a place where you can): I want to be an amazing teacher. I want people to be amazed by my teaching.

Does that sound like a goal you could embrace? Or, does it sound self-serving or egotistical? However it sounds I believe it is a goal every teacher should adopt: I want to be an amazing teacher; I want people to be amazed by my teaching.

We have too many teachers who are the opposite. Their teaching is very un-amazing. It is boring. Howard Hendricks said, "It is a sin to bore people with the gospel." If you teach the gospel and people are constantly looking at their watches, learn to teach like Jesus. His teaching was amazing. He got people talking. He created a buzz.

How did Jesus create this buzz?

Do not think I have come to bring peace?

Did Jesus come to bring peace on earth? Before you answer, consider this verse:

Luke 12:51 (ESV) Do you think that I have come to give peace on earth? No, I tell you, but rather division.

Should we do our good works so people can see them, or should we do them privately so no one can see?

Matthew 5:16 (ESV) In the same way, let your light shine before others, so that they may see your good works and give glory to your Father who is in heaven.

Is it sometimes appropriate to call someone a fool? Jesus called the Pharisees blind fools, which sounds even worse:

Matthew 23:17 (NIV) You blind fools! Which is greater: the gold, or the temple that makes the gold sacred?

OK, ready to answer? Before you do, consider these two verses:

- Matthew 6:1-4 (NIV) Be careful not to do your 'acts of righteousness' before men, to be seen by them. If you do, you will have no reward from your Father in heaven. So when you give to the needy, do not announce it with trumpets, as the hypocrites do in the synagogues and on the streets, to be honored by men. I tell you the truth, they have received their reward in full. But when you give to the needy, do not let your left hand know what your right hand is doing, so that your giving may be in secret. Then your Father, who sees what is done in secret, will reward you.

- John 14:27 (NIV) Peace I leave with you; my peace I give you. I do not give to you as the world gives. Do not let your hearts be troubled and do not be afraid.
- Matthew 5:22b (NIV) But anyone who says, 'You fool!' will be in danger of the fire of hell.

What's going on here?

Jesus spoke of the small gate. It is a small gate and it is easy to miss by bumping into the post on either side. He spoke of the narrow road. It is narrow because it is easy to fall off into one ditch or the other.

It is easy to fall into the ditch of doing your acts of righteousness before men to be seen by them. We have all seen that happen. It is also possible to be so secretive about your good works that no one knows and God receives no glory. God is only glorified when we do our acts of righteousness before men. We don't want to put our light under a bushel. Find the narrow way.

It is easy to fall into the ditch of believing that Jesus is all about "peace, peace." He is about that, but He is also about stirring things up, creating controversy and making division.

It is easy to fall into the ditch of thinking that God determines everything. After all, Jesus said, "You did not choose me." But, Jesus also said, "If anyone would come after me. . ." suggesting that it is up to us whether we come after him.

It is easy to fall into the ditch of believing we can lose our salvation. After all, the Bible says, "If we deny him, he will deny us." (2 Timothy 2.12 ESV) Jesus said, "No one can snatch them out of my Father's hand." John 10.29

What about calling someone a fool? What are we to make of the fact that Jesus said anyone who calls someone a fool is in danger of hell fire? Then, he went out and called the Pharisees fools (same Greek word).

Here is what I make of it. The Bible is not written in legaleze and should not be interpreted as legaleze. We do great damage to the Bible when we interpret it as legaleze. So much of the Bible falls under the heading, "Come, let us reason together." So often as I read the Bible I hear our Lord saying, "Just be reasonable."

By teaching both sides of the issue, Jesus' teaching was inherently interesting. It is this controversy or tension that makes it interesting. When something is a little difficult to understand, it creates intrigue. When there is mystery, there is intrigue.

Interesting thing about the teaching of Jesus: He never used the word balance. In fact, his teaching didn't seem very balanced. It seemed rather extreme. It seemed radical. When he taught about bringing a sword rather than peace, he didn't say, "Now, on the other hand, don't forget the balancing truth: peace I leave with you." When he said to let your light so shine before men, he didn't add the caveat that we need to be careful to not do this to bring attention to ourselves. When Jesus taught two sides of a balancing issue, he didn't try to resolve them. I recommend you do the same.

When you teach on Romans 9, teach like a Calvinist: "It does not, therefore, depend on man's desire or effort, but on God's mercy." Romans 9:16 (NIV) When you teach on 2 Timothy 2:12b —(NIV) "If we disown him, he will also disown us" — put the fear of God in them. Make John Wesley proud.

Teach like Jesus.

Slaves

John MacArthur argues strenuously and persuasively that we are slaves, not mere servants of Christ. Here is an excerpt: [30]

> *Scripture's prevailing description of the Christian's relationship to Jesus Christ is the slave/master relationship. But do a casual read through your English New Testament and you won't see it.*
>
> *The reason for this is as simple as it is shocking: the Greek word for slave has been covered up by being mistranslated in almost every English version—going back to both the King James Version and the Geneva Bible that predated it. Though the word slave (doulos in Greek) appears 124 times in the original text, it is correctly translated only once in the King James. Most of our modern translations do only slightly better. It almost seems like a conspiracy.*
>
> *Instead of translating doulos as "slave," these translations consistently substitute the word servant*

---

[30] MacArthur, John (2010). Slave: *The Hidden Truth About Your Identity in Christ (pp. 15-16).* Thomas Nelson. Kindle Edition.

in its place. Ironically, the Greek language has at least half a dozen words that can mean servant. The word doulos is not one of them. Whenever it is used, both in the New Testament and in secular Greek literature, it always and only means slave. According to the Theological Dictionary of the New Testament, a foremost authority on the meaning of Greek terms in Scripture, the word doulos is used exclusively "either to describe the status of a slave or an attitude corresponding to that of a slave." The dictionary continues by noting that:

the meaning is so unequivocal and self-contained that it is superfluous to give examples of the individual terms or to trace the history of the group. . . . [The] emphasis here is always on "serving as a slave." Hence we have a service which is not a matter of choice for the one who renders it, which he has to perform whether he likes it or not, because he is subject as a slave to an alien will, to the will of his owner. [The term stresses] the slave's dependence on his lord.

Convinced? Before you decide, consider the words of Jesus:

I do not call you slaves anymore, because a slave doesn't know what his master is doing. I have called you friends, because I have made known to you everything I have heard from My Father. John 15:15 (HCSB)

I use the Holman here because it is one translation that consistently translates the Greek word doulos as John MacArthur suggests, "slaves" rather than "servants" as it is in other translations. In this passage, Jesus seems to disagree with John MacArthur, saying that we are not slaves. Not even servants. Jesus has called us friends. I like that.

But, there are a lot of other verses where we are called slaves. James, for example, introduced himself as, "James, a slave of God and of the Lord Jesus Christ." James 1:1 (HCSB) (Interesting language coming from Jesus' brother.)

Paul used the same language is Romans 1:1, "Paul, a slave of Christ Jesus."

In our day the late Bill Bright is famous for having signed a contract to be a slave of Christ. He describes it in this way:

> Vonette and I each literally signed the contract with our Lord to be His slaves. We specified that we understood that He owned us and all we had. We surrendered our lives to His decision and control. I know now, with the benefit of hindsight, that this decision was merely a way for me to recognize the joy of what theologians call "spiritual slavery." It is the beginning of the outworking of the joy of our salvation (see Phil. 2:12). I journeyed from being the master of my own fate to realizing the enormity of God's love and incredible plan for my life and wanting to serve Him completely

and forever. I wanted to be a slave to such a wonderful Master![31]

Perhaps John MacArthur is right: "The gospel is not simply an invitation to become Christ's associate; it is a mandate to become His slave."[32]

Perhaps we would find the narrow way: both slaves and friends.

Teach like Jesus.

Blessed are the. . .

Question: Did Jesus mean, "In spite of the fact that you are poor in Spirit, you can still be blessed with the kingdom of heaven"? Or, did he mean, "Pursue being poor in spirit so that you can enter into the kingdom of heaven."

I never noticed until recently that the beatitudes take one of two forms.

---

[31] Bill Bright. *My Life Is Not My Own: Following God No Matter the Cost* (p. 34). Kindle Edition.

[32] MacArthur, John (2010). *Slave: The Hidden Truth About Your Identity in Christ* (p. 19). Thomas Nelson. Kindle Edition.

Beatitude form #1:

The first form of the beatitudes that I want to explore goes like this: In spite of condition "A" you can be blessed. The last beatitude clearly takes this form: In spite of the fact that you will be persecuted, you will be blessed. Jesus isn't suggesting that we pursue persecution; it will come on its own. In spite of the fact that persecution will come, we can find happiness.

I think the second beatitude has this form: "God blesses those who mourn, for they will be comforted." Matthew 5:4 (NLT). I don't think he is saying to pursue mourning—although some commentators do—I think he is saying, "In spite of the fact that life is hard and you will grieve, know that you will be comforted." You can find blessedness, or happiness.

Note: Happy is a synonym for blessed. The Today's English Version translates it that way, as does the New Century Version: "Happy are those. . ." When Kenneth Taylor prepared his paraphrase in the original Living Bible, he used the phrase, "How fortunate are the. . ." TDNT (Kittel) says, "It denotes the transcendent happiness of a life beyond care, labour and death."[33] Louw-Nida has, "pertaining to being happy, with the implication of enjoying favorable circumstances—'happy.'"[34] BAGD says, "blessed, fortunate, happy."[35] The word happy has fallen into disrespect in recent times, but it is a solidly biblical word. If you read the sermons of men of a previous generation, you find they used it all the time, as should we. Spurgeon used the word happy far more often than modern preachers, as did Jonathan Edwards and most preachers of previous generations. It is a recent phenomenon that Christians have gotten uncomfortable with the word happy.

Beatitude form #2:

This form is rather the opposite of form #1. Rather than "in spite of such and such condition," this one

---

[33] *Vol. 4: Theological dictionary of the New Testament.* 1964- (G. Kittel, G. W. Bromiley & G. Friedrich, Ed.) (electronic ed.) (362). Grand Rapids, MI: Eerdmans.

[34] Louw, J. P., & Nida, E. A. (1996). *Vol. 1: Greek-English lexicon of the New Testament : Based on semantic domains (electronic ed. of the 2nd edition.)* (301). New York: United Bible societies.

[35] Arndt, W., Gingrich, F. W., Danker, F. W., & Bauer, W. (1996). *A Greek-English lexicon of the New Testament and other early Christian literature : A translation and adaption of the fourth revised and augmented edition of Walter Bauer's Griechisch-deutsches Worterbuch zu den Schrift en des Neuen Testaments und der ubrigen urchristlichen Literatur* (486). Chicago: University of Chicago Press.

is almost a command to pursue the condition. The first form hints at avoiding a certain condition if you can, but since you won't always be able to, be comforted to know that you can still be blessed. This second form suggests we pursue it. We are to pursue hungering and thirsting after righteousness, and in that pursuit we will find satisfaction.

Most of the beatitudes take this form: Become pure in heart so that you can have the blessing of seeing God. Become a peacemaker and you will know the blessing of being called a son of God. Be merciful and you will receive mercy.

Here is the tricky part: into which category do you place the first beatitude? The translators of the NLT clearly put it into the second (pursue this) category: "God blesses those who are poor and realize their need for him, for the Kingdom of Heaven is theirs." Matthew 5:3 (NLT) It seems to me that they have over-translated and crossed the line from translation to commentary. The ESV is a more straightforward approach: "Blessed are the poor in spirit, for theirs is the kingdom of heaven." Matthew 5:3 (ESV)

It is said that the Bible is always the best commentary on the Bible. When we are faced with a difficult biblical question, the first thing we should ask is, "What other passages speak to this?" Fortunately, Jesus gave essentially this same sermon on another occasion, which Luke records in chapter 6. It is known as the Sermon on the Plain. The language is so similar in the beatitude section it is almost certain Jesus meant the same thing in both cases.

He meant the same thing, but he used different words: "Blessed are you who are poor, for yours is the kingdom of God." Luke 6:20 (NIV) Notice the words "in spirit" are omitted when Jesus gave the sermon this time. Here, he just said poor. The word means really poor—destitute, beggarly. I don't think Jesus is saying to pursue being really poor. He is saying that in spite of the fact that you might be poor, you can still find happiness.

He is right, by the way. And there is a lot of research today that demonstrates that money has very little to do with happiness. Happiness researcher Sonja Lyubomirsky says, "Very wealthy people have a great deal more than the average person, but the research shows that they are not much happier."[36]

---

[36] Lyubomirsky, Sonja (2007). *The How of Happiness* (p. 43). Penguin Press Hardcover. Kindle Edition.

So, when Jesus said, "Blessed are the poor in spirit" was he thinking of the humble or the monetarily poor? Was he saying "In spite of the fact that you are in a condition that you should avoid if you can (being poor), you can still find happiness." Or, was he saying, "Pursue humility and in humility you will be blessed"?

When Jesus said, "Blessed are those who mourn" did he mean that we should grieve for our sins, as is often preached, or did he mean, "In spite of the fact that painful times will come, you can find blessing in the comfort of God."?

Here is an even more important question: why did Jesus leave this open to doubt? This is arguably Jesus' most famous sermon; why wasn't Jesus more clear? Why did he leave himself open to various interpretations?

Before I answer that, let me point out one other thing: either interpretation yields a legitimate truth. You won't get yourself into trouble if you accept one interpretation over the other. This is an amazing thing, really. It is amazing that Jesus could make these simple, poetic statements that can be interpreted in two opposite ways and both ways yield a truth. Amazing.

But, it still begs the question: why not spell it out? Why did Jesus so often speak in such a way as to leave his words open to various interpretations? He surely could have spoken more clearly. He surely knew that whole denominations would split over various interpretations of his words. Surely he could have chosen words that would not be open to various interpretations. Why was Jesus sometimes (often?) confusing? I am not alone in noticing that Jesus was confusing. Brian McLaren asks, "Why did Jesus speak in parables? Why was he subtle, indirect, and secretive?"[37] Why was Jesus so confusing?

Why are the words of the Bible sometimes confusing and open to different translation and interpretation? Consider two classic verses. First, John 1:5. Question: what can the darkness never do to the light?

- John 1:5 (NIV) The light shines in the darkness, but the darkness has not understood it.
- John 1:5 (CEV) The light keeps shining in the dark, and darkness has never put it out.
- John 1:5 (GW) The light shines in the dark, and the dark has never extinguished it.

---

[37] McLaren, Brian D. (2007). The Secret Message of Jesus: Uncovering the Truth that Could Change Everything (p. 46). Thomas Nelson. Kindle Edition.

- John 1:5 (ESV) The light shines in the darkness, and the darkness has not overcome it.
- John 1:5 (HCSB) That light shines in the darkness, yet the darkness did not overcome it.
- John 1:5 (NASB) The Light shines in the darkness, and the darkness did not comprehend it.

Which is it? The darkness cannot comprehend/understand the light? Or, the darkness can never conquer the light. Here is the Josh Hunt translation: the darkness cannot grasp the light. This carries the double meaning. If you grasp the flame of a candle with your hand you will put it out. You can grasp an idea and understand it. Which one is meant? Why is the Bible so confusing?

One more: Romans 12:1:

- Romans 12:1 (NIV) Therefore, I urge you, brothers, in view of God's mercy, to offer your bodies as living sacrifices, holy and pleasing to God--this is your spiritual act of worship.
- Romans 12:1 (NKJV) I beseech you therefore, brethren, by the mercies of God, that you present your bodies a living sacrifice, holy, acceptable to God, *which is* your reasonable service.

Is the act of presenting our bodies to God a spiritual act of worship or a reasonable act of service? Here is the fine print. Logikos can be translated spiritual or reasonable. Latreia can be translated service and worship. (In the ancient mind worship and service were closely connected.)

Here is the question: there are other words the writer could have used. Why did they use these confusing ones that are open to interpretation? Why is the Bible so confusing?

Because confusing is intriguing. Confusing gets people talking. We are still arguing over Jesus words 2000 years later and I think Jesus wanted that. He knew that the most intriguing teaching is a little bit unclear.

Garrett Soden discusses this in his book, *Hook, Spin, Buzz*: "Part of what makes buzz vibrate is the friction between different interpretations of what the buzz is really about."[38]

We have talked about Kennedy's death for decades because we are not sure. Who was really behind it? Was it one lone kook, or was

---

[38] *Hook, Spin, Buzz*, Garrett Soden. P. 174

there a conspiracy? Was the CIA involved? Who knows? And it is this lack of understanding that makes it intriguing.

This is why political candidates don't just come out and say they are running for president. They hint for a long time. They make you wonder. They suggest long before they declare. They do things that look like a presidential candidate, but they don't actually declare themselves to be a candidate. This lack of clarity gets people talking. It creates a buzz as Jesus' teaching created a buzz.

What must I do to inherit eternal life?

It is always fascinating when Jesus answers a question in a way that we would never answer it. In fact, if we heard someone answer the way Jesus asked this question, we would likely correct them.

A man came to Jesus (Luke 18.18ff) and asked, "What must I do to have eternal life?" When you took evangelism training, how did they teach you to answer this question? What did they teach you not to say or do? Two things come to my mind:

- Don't change the subject. You have a live one here. Take it seriously. Pay attention. Don't let the conversation get off the subject.
- Communicate clearly that we are saved by grace through faith and not by works. The main thing is they understand we are not saved by works. Most people think we are saved by works. Make sure this is clear: we are not saved by works, but by grace acting through the conduit of faith. This is the trusting plan, not the trying plan.

How did Jesus respond? First he changed the subject. Not good. The man had included the word good in his salutation. Jesus picked up on that and asked why he called him good.

Then he answers the main question with this statement: "You know the commands. 'Do not commit adultery, do not murder, and so forth.'" He doesn't even mention the last and most difficult command: Do not covet.

If you were this man, what are you thinking? If I were this man, I would be thinking, "If I do the law I can get saved that way." Jesus potentially led this man to believe that he could be saved by obeying the law.

Can you be saved by obeying the law?

Yes.

But, you have to do it perfectly.

This gets into some theological water that is beyond the scope of our study. My point is this: Jesus' teaching was intriguing because it was open to misinterpretation. Jesus could have been misunderstood. Jesus intentionally spoke in such a way that he could be misunderstood. He was not crystal clear.

Do you disagree? Would you like me to explain more? Jesus' teaching often left people with that feeling. Teach like Jesus.

No one was neutral

I write a curriculum for groups called Good Questions Have Groups Talking. For me, honestly, it is a marketing slogan. "Have groups talking" was more than a marketing slogan for Jesus. It was his normal. Jesus always had people talking. Look at the variety in which this word "whispering" is translated: [emphasis added.]

- John 7:12 (NIV) Among the crowds there was widespread **whispering** about him.

Some said, "He is a good man." Others replied,"No, he deceives the people."

- John 7:12 (CEV) The crowds **even got into an argument** about him. Some were saying, "Jesus is a good man," while others were saying, "He is lying to everyone."
- John 7:12 (GW) The crowds **argued** about Jesus. Some people said, "He's a good man," while others said, "No he isn't. He deceives the people."
- John 7:12 (ESV) And there was much **muttering** about him among the people. While some said, "He is a good man," others said, "No, he is leading the people astray."
- John 7:12 (NASB) There was much **grumbling** among the crowds concerning Him; some were saying, "He is a good man"; others were saying, "No, on the contrary, He leads the people astray."
- John 7:12 (HCSB) And there was **a lot of discussion** about Him among the crowds. Some were saying, "He's a good man." Others were saying, "No, on the contrary, He's deceiving the people."
- John 7:12 (MSG) There was a lot of **contentious talk** about him circulating through the crowds. Some were saying, "He's a good man." But others said, "Not so. He's selling snake oil."
- John 7:12 (NLT) There was a lot of **grumbling** about him among the crowds. Some argued, "He's a good man," but others said, "He's nothing but a fraud who deceives the people."

- John 7:12 (TEV) There was much **whispering** about him in the crowd. "He is a good man," some people said. "No," others said, "he fools the people."
- John 7:12 (NKJV) And there was much **complaining** among the people concerning Him. Some said, "He is good"; others said, "No, on the contrary, He deceives the people."

The word is used only four times in the New Testament. In the ESV it is translated three different ways. It is a fun word to say and sounds like what it means. Say it three times out loud and you will see what I mean: gongýzō. Grammarians call that an onomatopoeia. Murmur is also an onomatopoeia, as is grumbling. It sounds like what it means.

This word is one of seven that are translated "amazement." It seems the writers really made use of a thesaurus to describe people's reaction to Jesus' teaching.[39]

---

[39] Copyright Faithlife Corporation, makers of Logos Bible Software – www.logos.com

θαυμάζω
wonder, be amazed

θαμβέω
be astounded

ἔκστασις
amazement; ecstasy

θαυμαστός
wonderful

ἐκθαμβέω
be excited

γίνομαι + θάμβος
be born, become; amazement,
awe

amazement

ἐξίστημι
confuse; amaze

Jesus stirred things up. The people clapped. They gasped. They whispered. They yelled. They talked. Their mouths dropped open in silence. No one looked at their watches.

I don't know about you, but this is an inspiration and a challenge to me. I have to say my teaching doesn't get people talking like Jesus' did. On a good day they stay awake and they don't look at their watches too much. When it is done they smile and they politely shake my hand and say, "good job." I never read of anyone nodding and politely shaking Jesus' hand and saying, "good job."

I want to teach more like Jesus.

Kid-friendly

First century Palestine was a dangerous place to be a child. "Only about half of those children born lived beyond the age of eight, in part because of widespread infanticide, with famine and illness also being factors."[40]

Life was cheap back in the day. There was a classic line recorded in a letter from a man to his wife. His name was Hilarion, hers was Alis. The letter is dated 1 B.C. Notice how casual he is about killing his son:

> "Hilarion to Alis his wife heartiest greetings, and to my dear Berous and Apollonarion. Know that we tire still even now in Alexandria. Do not worry if when all others return I remain in Alexandria. I beg and beseech of you to take care of the little child, and, as soon as we receive wages, I will send them to you. If-- good luck to you!--you have a child, if it is a boy, let it live; if it is it girl, throw it out. You told Aphrodisias to tell me: 'Do not forget me.' How can I forget you? I beg you therefore not to worry." [41]

---

[40] Kennedy, D. James (2005). *What if Jesus had never been born?* (Kindle Locations 245-246). Thomas Nelson. Kindle Edition.

[41] *Barclay's Daily Study Bible (NT).*

It is hard for us to imagine such a callous attitude toward a precious child. But, in that day, the words precious and child were two words that would never be heard in the same sentence.

The words recorded by Hilarion above don't sound too different from the words of the king of Egypt, "When you help the Hebrew women in childbirth and observe them on the delivery stool, if it is a boy, kill him; but if it is a girl, let her live." Exodus 1.16 NIV

They came by this attitude honestly. They had a long history of abusing children. Children were considered property, and a father could dispose of them in any way and for any reason he chose:

> *Abandonment was commonplace: It was common for infirm babies or unwanted little ones to be taken out into the forest or the mountainside, to be consumed by wild animals or to starve or to be picked up by rather strange people who crept around at night, who then would use them for whatever perverted purposes they had in mind. Parents abandoned virtually all deformed babies. Many parents abandoned babies if they were poor. They often abandoned female babies because women were considered inferior.* [42]

---

[42] Kennedy, D. James (2005). *What if Jesus had never been born?* (Kindle Locations 239-243). Thomas Nelson. Kindle Edition.

In earlier generations, children were often sacrificed to the gods. Near a temple in Samaria, excavators found a graveyard just a few steps from the temple. In it they found many jars containing remains of human infants. This is what they did in the name of religion.

A low view of children was a part of a global world view that had a low view of man. Jewish thought and later Christianity saw man as the crowning achievement of God's creation. Created in the image of God, people of all ages were to be prized and respected. The ancient world never heard of human rights. "The individual was regarded as valuable only if he was a part of the political fabric and able to contribute to its uses, as though it were the end of his being to aggrandize the State."[43]

Every culture has its traditions with regard to children. We have baby showers and birthday parties. "It was a Roman custom to place a newborn on the ground in front of the father for him to inspect. When the father lifted the child, it symbolized the child's acceptance into the family

---

[43] Richard Frothingham, *The Rise of the Republic of the United States* (Boston: Little, Brown, 1910), 6. Quoted from: Schmidt, Alvin J. (2009). How Christianity Changed the World (p. 76). Zondervan. Kindle Edition.

(the Latin verb suscipere, "to lift up," came to mean "survival"). Weak, handicapped, unwanted girls, or another unwanted mouth to feed, would be left on the ground with the implication that the child should be exposed. Exposure was the practice of leaving an unwanted child at a site, usually a garbage dump or dung heap, where the child either died or was taken by a stranger to be raised, usually as a slave. Such infanticide practices were never sanctioned but never condemned by Roman law."[44]

This explains, by the way, a passage in scripture that would have been very troubling to us, but did not seem like much of a shocker to them. I refer to the story where Herod kills all the babies in the area that were under two years old. Barclay estimates that this may have been twenty or thirty babies. Can you imagine twenty or thirty babies being killed by a governor in our day? Can you imagine the scandal?

But, back in the day, this was not big news. It was sad, but it was not big news. This explains why we don't have any record of this event in secular

---

[44] Porter, S. E., & Evans, C. A. (2000). *Dictionary of New Testament background : A compendium of contemporary biblical scholarship* (electronic ed.). Downers Grove, IL: InterVarsity Press.

history. It was, in a way, all in a day's work for Herod. Herod was a mean man and children were an easy target of his meanness.

Jesus and children

It is in this context that we read, "Now they were bringing even infants to him that he might touch them. And when the disciples saw it, they rebuked them." Luke 18:15 (ESV) Note the word "even." Even the babies! It has the sense of, "Can you believe it? Babies!?"

The word Dr. Luke uses here describes an infant. It is the word Peter uses in 1 Peter 2:2 (NIV) "Like newborn babies, crave pure spiritual milk, so that by it you may grow up in your salvation." It is the word Elizabeth used of her unborn baby leaping in her womb. (Luke 1.44) These were babies. People in that day didn't value babies.

The disciples shooed them away. The verbs here indicate that they kept coming and coming the disciples kept shooing and shooing. Mark records that Jesus was indignant. It is a strong word. Jesus was mad. Vine says it is, "to feel a violent irritation, physically."[45] He was ticked.

And in his anger, Jesus calls the children to him and says, "Let the little children come to me, and do not hinder them, for the kingdom of God belongs to such as these." Luke 18:16 (NIV) Everyone else was pushing the children aside; Jesus called them to himself. Instead of being too busy for the children, Jesus made time for the children. Rather than excluding the children, Jesus included the children.

And Jesus gave us a command that we would do well to think soberly about as we think about our teaching: do not hinder the children.

Why we shouldn't hinder children

Children today are hurting. Barna reports:[46]

> One out of every 3 children born in the United States each year is born to an unmarried woman. One out of every 4 children presently lives with a single parent,

---

[45] Vine, W. E., Unger, M. F., & White, W. (1996). *Vine's Complete Expository Dictionary of Old and New Testament Words.* Nashville, TN: T. Nelson.

[46] Barna, George (2003-11-01). *Transforming Children into Spiritual Champions* (pp. 22-23). Gospel Light Publications. Kindle Edition.

and about half find themselves in that situation before they celebrate their eighteenth birthday. Three out of every 5 mothers of infants are in the labor force— roughly twice the proportion from just a quarter-century ago.

We ought to care for children because children are hurting. My wife teaches in a public school. The stories she comes home with are both amazing and depressing. Two eighth graders caught on tape having oral sex in the school cafeteria. One of her eighth grade girls is pregnant. Another doesn't know what happened to her dad, but she does know her mom is pregnant. They don't know who that father is. She says she got drunk last night. Almost all of these children have divorced parents. children are hurting today.

Love children like Jesus

Imagine a church that was, in the words of one writer, "The best hour in a kids life." Imagine a church where kids love to come. Imagine a church where kids counted down the days until Sunday because they couldn't wait to come to church. What would we have to do to make that dream come true? Here are a few ideas:

- **Notice kids.** Loving kids is the job of every one in the church, not just the children's workers. How often do kids walk right by us and we never see them, notice them or acknowledge them. We would never do that with an adult. We have the good sense to realize it is plain rude. But, with kids, we do it all the time. Don't. Notice kids. Pay attention to them. Acknowledge them.

It is interesting to me that commands about how we greet one another make it into the Bible. We tend to not notice these commands because we get caught up in the cultural disconnect when the Bible says to greet one another with a holy kiss. Ewwww! The point is this: it is important that we greet one another. Allow me to confess my own sin: I have hurt people because I did not greet them appropriately. I didn't intend to be mean. I am a bit of an air-head and have been known to just walk by people and never notice they existed. I hurt them. I want to do better. I want you to do better too—with adults and kids. Greet them. Notice them. Acknowledge them.

- **Touch kids appropriately.** The key word, of course, is appropriately. Don't ever let anyone accuse you of being inappropriate. But, don't let the fear of accusation keep you from touching kids lovingly and appropriately.

- **Learn kids' names.** The favorite word for everyone on planet earth is their own name. Learn kids' names and address them by name.
- **Ask about their lives**. Do they play soccer? Are they into XBox? What are their favorite games? What are their favorite movies? Ask.
- **Show up for their events.** Want to really make an impression on a kid? Show up at their soccer game. Show up for their play.
- **Provide the best programming you can for the kids.** When I was growing up we could get away with some pretty boring programming for kids. Sunday School and VBS didn't have to be spectacular to get kids to show up. The reason: we had a generation of parents that made kids attend. That generation has passed.

Many bemoan this passing. They like to pine for the good old days of *Leave It to Beaver* when everyone went to church. Get over it. Many churches have seen this as an opportunity. They provide programming that is the best hour in the kids' lives. Bill Hybels says that even unchurched people will bring their kids to church if the kids want to go. Willowcreek, and a whole generation of churches, make kids programming so interesting the kids drag the parents to church.

Want a real example of one church doing it right? Consider Northpoint. Here is how Andy Stanley describes their children's ministry:

Our goal was to make our environments so irresistible that even people who didn't buy our theology would want to come back and participate. As a result of God's favor and a whole lot of off-sites and hard work, we've been able to accomplish just that. Our family ministry environments are so magnetic, I warn people in our community not to bring their kids to our church until they're sure they want to attend on a regular basis. When they ask why, I tell them that once their kids "come and see" the environments we've created for them, they'll never be satisfied anywhere else. I assure them that I'm not being arrogant. I just don't want to make their Sunday mornings any harder than they already are.[47]

Jesus' teaching was kid-friendly. Our churches should be kid-friendly too.

Teach like Jesus.

---

[47] Stanley, A. (2012). *Deep and wide: Creating churches unchurched people love to attend*. Grand Rapids, MI: Zondervan.

Example

Jesus never taught anything he didn't live. He lived the life he called people to live. He prayed. His disciples saw him pray. They asked, "Teach us to pray." When he taught them to pray, he didn't get real elaborate. He didn't need to. He already lived it before them. They didn't need a lot of explanation to learn to do what they had seen him do. Jesus taught by example. Hybels calls these the most powerful two words Jesus ever spoke: "Follow me."[48]

The classic case of Jesus being an example is in John 13. Notice the irony in these words:

> Jesus knew that the Father had put all things under his power, and that he had come from God and was returning to God; so he got up from the meal, took off his outer clothing, and wrapped a towel around his waist. After that, he poured water into a basin and began to wash his disciples' feet, drying them with the towel that was wrapped around him. John 13:3-5 (NIV)

Imagine the President getting up from a presidential meal—perhaps one where he

---

[48] *Axiom*, Bill Hybels.

has entertained foreign presidents or key congressional leaders. Maybe he has entertained a rock star or movie mogul in the white house. Dinner is winding down. The President stands up, puts on a robe to cover his tuxedo, and begins to clear the dishes. "Are you through with that plate?"

Shocking.

Perhaps I should have included this piece under the section *Unexpected*, for this was certainly unexpected. But what I want to point out in this context is that Jesus taught by example. He never taught people to do things he was not doing.

When Jesus wanted to teach on servanthood, he didn't develop a really cool PowerPoint presentation. He didn't write a speech. He orchestrated a context where he could set an example. The example was one everyone was familiar with. The combination of dusty roads and open sandals would leave your feet as dirty as the hands of a potter. The foot washing was customarily done by a slave. This job was considered too menial to be done by a Jewish slave. The fact that it was not done would have created what we call an elephant in the room. There was this thing. It just hung there. Everyone knew it. They felt it. They felt their dirty feet and wanted them washed, as was the custom. They could have done it, but they were not about to. Perhaps Peter looked around and nodded an unspoken gesture to John to do something.

Remember that the disciples were not sitting at a table as we do. They were reclining at the table. The tables were short—perhaps 18 inches high. People would recline at a 45 degree angle from the table. A servant had easy access to the feet, but there was no servant. There was a conversation about who knows what but everyone knew what was on everyone's mind: where is the servant?

Jesus doesn't give a speech on servanthood. (Not that he would never do that. On another day, he does.) When he heard the disciples arguing about who would be the greatest, he even used an object lesson. He brought a child to his side and talked about how whoever is the least is the greatest. It wasn't time for another speech. This lesson—the lesson of servanthood—was central to what Jesus wanted to communicate and he needed to make it stick. He set an example for them to follow. He did what none of them would ever do in a million years. He washed their feet.

Foot washing was not a religious ritual. It was a common act of servanthood. It was like washing the dishes. It was like cleaning the table. It was like doing the laundry. It was doing what needed to be done.

Bruce Wilkinson said, "The teacher of God is the living link between the Word of God and the people of God."

Learning to be snake handlers

Imagine you were given this teaching assignment: teach people with a snake phobia (Ophidiophobia) that many snakes are safe. But, the learning objective is that as a result of your teaching, they would be able to calmly rest a large snake on their shoulders, allowing it to kiss their cheek if it desires. How would you teach this lesson?

This was precisely Dr. Albert Bandura's goal. He ran an ad in the Palo Alto news asking people who had a paralyzing fear of snakes to descend into the basement of the psychology department to receive their healing. What did they find there? A speech? Slick 4-color brochures? A presentation?

Mind you, these were people with serious ophidiophobia. Their fears were as debilitating as they were unreasonable. "Most had horrible nightmares, many were veritable shut-ins, and since their irrational fear extended to even harmless garter snakes, the possible subjects suffered endless ridicule and indignity."[49]

How do you teach people like that to handle snakes? What if we upped the ante? What if we said you had to get it done in three hours? What would you do?

Bandura asked snake-phobics to watch people handle snakes. (Many of these people couldn't even be in the same room as the snake handlers did their thing.) They watched and breathed. Slowly, their heart started pounding a little slower. Their hands got a little less sweaty and their mouth a little less dry. They took a step closer. They paused. They breathed. They took another step. By the time they stepped into the same room as the snakes, some had to wear hockey gear and similar protection. They kept watching the example of the snake handler. They kept getting a little closer. Eventually they could touch the cage where the snake was held. Eventually

---

[49] Switzler, Al (2007). *Influencer : The Power to Change Anything* (p. 46). McGraw-Hill. Kindle Edition.

they could put their hand in the cage. Eventually they could hold the snake. It only took three hours. Three hours. It started with an example.

Jimmy Carter teaches the world to build houses

Jimmy Carter has long been an advocate for the poor and the homeless. He could get elected president and be an advocate for the homeless. He could give speeches and lead congress to pass laws. He did that. He could influence the federal budget to help providing low income housing. He did that. What else could he do?

He could set an example.

Bill Hybels talks about how Jimmy Carter did this:

> *Former president Jimmy Carter did this as well as any leader I've ever seen. After his term as president of the United States, he desperately wanted Americans to catch the vision of providing quality housing for under-resourced people. Rather than immediately hitting the speaking circuit, he and his wife, Rosalyn, bought hammers and started hitting nails for Habitat for Humanity.* [50]

---

[50] Hybels, Bill (2009). *Courageous Leadership* (Kindle Locations 473-475). Zondervan. Kindle Edition.

Hybels reduces it to a slogan: The leader must embody the vision.

Andy Stanley and Northpoint: how to lead groups to double

Andy Stanley and Northpoint church is the best example I know of a church that has grown through multiplying groups. Their publicly stated vision: "We envision fifty thousand people participating in weekly small groups that are committed to multiplying."[51] This is a story I have watched pretty closely because my most popular book and conference is about how to double a group in two years or less. Northpoint is the best example I know of a church that is doing it.

How is Andy leading toward having 50,000 in multiplying groups? Talks? Logic? Verbal arguments? Yes, but the real weapon is example:

> *Your willingness to embody the vision of your organization will have a direct impact on your credibility as a leader. Living out the vision establishes credibility and makes you a leader worth following. When people are convinced that the vision has stuck with you, it is easier for them to make the effort to stick with the vision. Your giftedness may enable you to*

---

[51] Stanley, Andy (2009). *Making Vision Stick* (Kindle Location 146). Zondervan. Kindle Edition.

gather a following. But it will take more than talent to make your vision stick.

When you embody the vision of your organization, people come to believe that your job is more than just a job for you. Over time it occurs to insiders that you would be doing the same thing even if there weren't an organization to support you. When it is evident to those closest to you that you have personally embraced the vision, you give them permission to do the same. At that point you're not leading from position—you're leading from influence. Living out the vision establishes credibility and makes you a leader worth following. When people are convinced that the vision has stuck with you, it is easier for them to make the effort to stick with the vision.

When my wife, Sandra, and I bring an unchurched friend or family to a weekend service, I tell the staff about it on Monday morning. I thank them for partnering with my family to reach our community. I talk about our small group. I look for opportunities to talk about the difference our children's small groups are making on our kids. I want them to know that this is personal for me. I believe. I'm in. This isn't just a job. It's a calling.

If you say you believe in something, live it out. And live it in a way that the people around you can see it. That's not arrogant. That's liberating. [52]

---

[52] Stanley, Andy (2009). *Making Vision Stick* (Kindle Locations 356-357). Zondervan. Kindle Edition.

Whatever you want people to do, you must do. Teach by example.

This was Jesus' complaint against the Pharisees: "For they don't practice what they teach." Matthew 23.3 NLT

Teach like Jesus.

Just teach

How much time do you think Jesus spent in what we call sermon preparation? Do you think Jesus studied as an average pastor studied? Do you think he read, did research, prepared outlines and so forth? How much time do you imagine Jesus spent preparing to teach?

In a way, I think that is all Jesus did. I think he was constantly thinking about how to communicate what the kingdom was about.

By the way, the most common message in many churches is about this question: how can we know we will go to heaven when we die? Jesus rarely talked about that. He mostly talked about the kingdom. Think about that for a bit. When you are finished, keep reading.

I imagine Jesus' mind was constantly churning with the question: how can I communicate with them about what the kingdom is like? Every time he saw some birds or observed a farmer or went to the temple, he was thinking about how to communicate the message of the temple.

When he taught, many times, he just taught. No outlines. No alliterations. No three points and a poem. He just taught.

If you have a red letter edition of the Bible, thumb through the gospels. There are sections where you have paragraph after paragraph of red letters. Sometimes, it is page after page. If you look closer you find a hodge-podge of mostly unrelated thoughts. Unrelated, except they revolve around one theme: the kingdom of God.

Evidence that Jesus was constantly ruminating about the kingdom of God comes from the fact that it seemed to erupt from Jesus spontaneously. His disciples realized they had forgotten to bring some bread to eat. Jesus mind goes to bread . . . yeast . . . he erupts, "'Watch out!' Jesus warned them. "Beware of the yeast of the Pharisees and Sadducees." Matthew 16:6 (NLT) Jesus once saw a fig tree. He thought about fruitfulness. He examines the fig tree. No fruit. "Ah ha!" he thinks! "Perfect example!"

Sometimes Jesus just lectured. Years ago, Dan Baumann wrote a book called *All originality makes a dull church.* What he was getting at was this. If you constantly have to one-up yourself with something bigger, something snazzier, something better, something more spectacular. . . after a while it just gets wearisome. Somewhere along the line, normal ought to be good enough. A lot of Jesus' teaching was normal. It was just talking. No tear-jerking story. No side-splitting laughter. Some of that is good. A little goes a long way.

Years ago I read an article in Leadership Magazine called Raisins in the Oatmeal: How to illustrate a sermon. The main content of a message is the oatmeal; the illustrations are the raisins. We do well not to reverse it.

Illustrations are like special effects in a movie. I love a movie with great special effects. It is what made the Star Trek series as well as the Star Wars movies. They were always on the cutting edge for their day with special effects. But, a movie built on special effects alone will only hold the attention of Jr. High boys. They like to see things blow up enough to sit through it. The rest of us want to see a plot.

A message that just has one story after another is not likely to hold an audience. There needs to be a story that holds the whole thing together. Thumb through the gospels in a red letter edition. You will find places where there is paragraph after paragraph without a story. Much of the Sermon on the Mount is that way.

Jesus' teaching was not only interesting because he said it in an interesting way; it was fundamentally interesting because he had something interesting to say.

The best teachers you have heard are this way. You sat spellbound, not because they had great speaking technique, but because they had a message.

If you notice the technique of the teacher it is a sure sign that the teacher is not exceptional. With exceptional teachers you just get lost in the message.

There comes a time to forget about being creative and just teach.

Pick up a book you consider a great Christian book. For me that might be *The Holiness of God* by Sproul, J.I. Packer's *Knowing God*, Piper's *Desiring God*, or anything by John Ortberg. Highlight the stories. You will likely find there are quite a few. But, it is not all stories. Much of it is just interesting prose.

There comes a time to just teach.

Easy to understand; impossible to fathom

When Jesus' disciples asked him to teach them to pray, he didn't give fourteen principles on prayer. He didn't give them a book. He didn't even give them a sermon. He gave them a very short, simple, prayer.

> *One day Jesus was praying in a certain place. When he finished, one of his disciples said to him, "Lord, teach us to pray, just as John taught his disciples." He said to them, "When you pray, say: "'Father, hallowed be your name, your kingdom come. Give us each day our daily bread. Forgive us our sins, for we also forgive everyone who sins against us. And lead us not into temptation.'"*
> *Luke 11:1–4 (NIV)*

Thirty four words in the NIV. Simple.

Is your teaching simple? Teach like Jesus.

Many are enamored with deep teaching—big words and long charts and "the Greek says" and all that. Jesus was enamored with simple. I am

153

fond of saying, "We teach so little because we teach so much." I am fond of a one point sermon. A fourteen point sermon probably won't be understood by anyone. Andy Stanley says it even more briefly: "Less is more."

Jesus' teaching was clear. It was simple. Crisp. You didn't have to wonder what he meant. When Jesus said, "Do to others what you would have them do to you" people didn't scratch their heads and wonder what he meant. They didn't discuss or debate. His teaching was clear.

However.

Jesus' teaching was not always that simple. We are still scratching our heads about much of his teaching. People are still debating. We still disagree. Let's look at two examples.

> *Mark 4:11-12 (NIV) He told them, "The secret of the kingdom of God has been given to you. But to those on the outside everything is said in parables so that, 'they may be ever seeing but never perceiving, and ever hearing but never understanding; otherwise they might turn and be forgiven!'"*

This passage is not actually difficult to understand. That is what is troubling about it. It is pretty clear what Jesus is saying: "I speak in parables so it will be confusing to many. If I didn't do this everyone would understand, repent, believe and be forgiven. I don't want everyone to turn and be forgiven." Of course, if your Calvinism is strong enough, you might think that is exactly what Jesus had in mind. The rest of us are a little confused.

Example two.

> *John 6:53-56 (NIV) Jesus said to them, "I tell you the truth, unless you eat the flesh of the Son of Man and drink his blood, you have no life in you. Whoever eats my flesh and drinks my blood has eternal life, and I will raise him up at the last day. For my flesh is real food and my blood is real drink. Whoever eats my flesh and drinks my blood remains in me, and I in him."*

What exactly does that mean? Here is how one commentator explains it:

> *What follows is a paragraph which must be understood spiritually. It tells us first that spiritual appropriation provides initial life. Without the careful textual approach, we can end up with some kind of theological cannibalism. Jesus was talking about the cross—the spiritual act whereby we accept his death on our behalf in order to gain access to his offer of eternal life. In the spiritual sense, that is the real food and the real drink. — Holman New Testament Commentary – John.*

Did you work all that out on your first reading of the passage?

Here is the real question—why did Jesus leave this lack of clarity in his teaching? Surely he could have made it so clear that there was no debate. Why did Jesus teach in such a way that 2000 years later we are not clear—and not agreed on what He said? Why did he leave his teaching open to interpretation?

Jesus did this quite often. I'd challenge you to read through the gospels with this in mind: look for every time Jesus' teaching was less than completely clear. It happened all the time. Why?

Recall these words quoted earlier:

> *The ideas in buzz can be described, but not defined.*
> *Part of what makes buzz vibrate is the friction between*
> *different interpretations of what the buzz is really*
> *about.*[53] *(Italics added)*

The way to get people talking is to be just a little controversial. Don't be completely clear. Let people misunderstand. People will walk away arguing. . .

---

[53] *Webster's New Collegiate Dictionary*, (Springfield, Massachusetts: G. & C. Merriam Company, 1979) p. 888.

- Did he say. . .
- I thought he meant. . .
- That can't possibly be right. I think. . .

You know you have done this well as a teacher when people come up to you days later and say, "I have been thinking about what we talked about and I think. . ."

Stepping back a bit from Jesus' teaching and looking at the teaching of the Bible as a whole we see this all through the Bible. God intentionally made the Bible unclear in places so people would argue, people would debate, churches would split and denominations would be born.

God's sovereignty and man's moral responsibility

The classic example of this tension is in the issue of God's sovereignty and man's moral responsibility. I remember reading this passage for the first time. Talk about a shocker:

> Romans 9:14-18 (NIV) What then shall we say? Is God unjust? Not at all! [15] For he says to Moses, "I will have mercy on whom I have mercy, and I will have compassion on whom I have compassion." [16] It does not, therefore, depend on man's desire or effort, but on God's mercy. [17] For the Scripture says to Pharaoh: "I raised you up for this very purpose, that I might

*display my power in you and that my name might be
proclaimed in all the earth." ¹⁸ Therefore God has mercy
on whom he wants to have mercy, and he hardens
whom he wants to harden.*

It seemed to contradict passages I was more
familiar with:

*2 Peter 3:9 (NIV) The Lord is not slow in keeping his
promise, as some understand slowness. He is patient
with you, not wanting anyone to perish, but everyone
to come to repentance.*

*John 3:16 (NIV) For God so loved the world that he
gave his one and only Son, that whoever believes in
him shall not perish but have eternal life.*

We are not going to settle this debate here.
Theologians have been arguing for years and
they will be arguing on the day the trumpet
sounds.

There is another thing they will be arguing about.
They will be arguing about pre-mil, post-mil (my
favorite; I follow R.C. Sproul on this), a-mil, pre-trib,
mid-trib, post-trib. . . until That Day.

They argue about baptism. They argue about
church organization: elders or no? They argue
about speaking in tongues. They argue about
women in ministry.

They argue in print. They argue over the internet. They argue in pulpits. They argue in Starbucks.

But here is one place they don't argue. They don't argue in the average Sunday School class. They don't argue in the average small group. We are way too polite. What our classes need is a few more arguments—no; what we need is a lot more arguments.

The truth of God is bigger than any of us really understand and the tension is built into the text. Jesus said, "Let your light so shine before men. . ." and, "Be careful not to do your acts of righteousness to be seen of men." Which is it? Let's have a debate. Let's argue. Let's disagree.

Teach like Jesus.

Do you disagree with me? Do you want to argue with me? Do you want to correct me?

Send them out to do

We learn by doing. We don't learn by hearing. We need to hear but we never learn if all we do is hear. We must do. That is why Jesus' brother told us to be doers of the word and not hearers only (James 1.22). He went on to say that if we merely listen to the Word and don't do anything, we actually deceive ourselves.

We deceive ourselves because we think we are getting better when we are not. We deceive ourselves. We come to church. We hear the sermons. We come to Bible Study. We listen. We even participate. We discuss. We might even memorize and study the Bible on our own. All of it is wood, hay and stubble if we don't do one more thing. We must do something.

We learn by doing.

Jesus' teaching had a bias toward action. He didn't want people to sit and soak. He didn't want them

to just hear and soak it in. He wanted them to do
Consider these verses.

> *John 7:17 (NIV) If anyone chooses to do God's will, he
> will find out whether my teaching comes from God or
> whether I speak on my own.*

> *John 13:17 (NIV) Now that you know these things, you
> will be blessed if you do them.*

> *Matthew 7:21 (NIV) "Not everyone who says to me,
> 'Lord, Lord,' will enter the kingdom of heaven, but only
> he who does the will of my Father who is in heaven."*

> *Matthew 7:24 (NIV) "Therefore everyone who hears
> these words of mine and puts them into practice is like
> a wise man who built his house on the rock."*

> *Matthew 25:40 (NIV) "The King will reply, 'I tell you the
> truth, whatever you did for one of the least of these
> brothers of mine, you did for me.'"*

He didn't admonish people to hear about God's
will or study God's will or even understand God's
will. He spoke of doing God's will. He didn't say
we would be blessed if we hear these things
or understand these things or memorize these
things. Rather, he says we will be blessed if we do
these things.

Jesus taught that doing—not just believing in—the will of the Father was the doorway to the Kingdom. The wise man puts wise words into practice. Jesus had a bias for action.

Herman Horne lists twenty five separate times Jesus taught people by telling them to do something:[54]

1. "Come."
2. "Follow."
3. "Go."
4. "Sell."
5. "Preach."
6. "Watch."
7. "Pray."
8. "Do likewise."
9. "Wash."
10. "Offer the gift."
11. "Stretch out your hand."
12. "Take away the stone."
13. "Come down."
14. "Go and tell."
15. "Sin no more."
16. "Feed my sheep."
17. "Make disciples of all nations."
18. "Find a donkey."
19. "Give to Caesar."
20. "Show yourself to the priest."
21. "Get up, take your mat."
22. "Give them something to eat."

[54] Herman Horne. *Jesus the Teacher: Examining His Expertise in Education* (pp. 121-122). Kindle Edition

23. "Work."
24. "Make them come in."
25. "Turn to him the other [cheek]."

Jesus constantly told his disciples to do something. Teach like Jesus.

If you want to teach people to pray, get them praying. If you want to teach them to serve, get them serving. If you want to teach them to study their Bibles, get them studying their Bibles. If you want to teach them to witness, get them witnessing. We learn by doing.

Here is a quote from Will Rogers that you wouldn't expect to find in a Christian book: "There are three kinds of men, ones that learn by reading, a few who learn by observation, and the rest of them have to pee on the electric fence and find out for themselves."[55]

This is why Jesus sent the disciples out. They had heard enough; it was time to do something. "He sent them out to proclaim the kingdom of God." Luke 9.2.

---

[55] Switzler, Al (2007-08-22). *Influencer : The Power to Change Anything* (p. 45). McGraw-Hill. Kindle Edition.

You might think Jesus sent his disciples out to preach as a benefit to the people who heard them. Certainly it was a benefit to them. But Jesus didn't seem too concerned about getting his message to wider and wider audiences. He seemed more concerned with getting his message more deeply into the hearts of his followers.

I don't think Jesus sent the disciples out for what it would do for the people in the cities he sent them to. He sent them out for the good that it would do the disciples. He knew that by them doing—preaching and healing—they would be transformed by what they did.

We see this all the time. As I write this I am on a mission trip. We are helping the Baptist Children's home in Portales, New Mexico. Hopefully, we will do some good for the home. Hopefully, we will show the kids some love. But here is what I know. The people who go on this trip will receive as much benefit as the kids at the home. I once heard a pastor say that he sees as much progress in discipleship in a one-week mission trip as he does in years of sitting in discipleship classes. Did you get that? One week on a mission trip accomplishes as much discipleship as one year in a classroom!

Bruce Wilkinson said that teachers are out of step with the purposes of God when they teach merely to "know."[56]

How the communist party converted half the world in one century

It is kind of old news now. We think of communism as a failed human experiment. We all saw the Berlin wall fall.

However, the spread of the belief in communism is an interesting study in how people are taught and how ideas spread. Communism spread to nearly half the world in less than half a century— this with an idea that was destined to fail. Imagine what they could have done if they had the truth!

How did they do it? One key component was they got early recruits out doing something. They didn't just sit in class learning about the communist party. They got them out doing something— passing out flyers, participating in fund raisers— anything to get them moving.

---

[56] Wilkinson, Bruce. (1992). *Seven Laws of the Learner* (pg 141). Colorado Springs, CO: Multnomah Books.

How to teach people not to hoard

I am trying to incorporate these principles into my own preaching and teaching. Recently, I preached on materialism. James actually uses the term made popular by a TV show: *Hoarders*. (James 5.3) I talked about how we all have a little hoarder in us. I showed a clip from the show. I explained what I could from the passage. Then, I asked people to do something. Give something— anything—away. Give something small away. Give something you don't need away. Give anything away. What is amazing is this: no matter how small the step, people struggle to take it.

Small seems to be the key to good application. Try to get people to do something—no matter how small or seemingly insignificant.

I read one book on hoarders and the writer had an interesting illustration. She asked one man to get rid of a coffee maker. Curious thing; he didn't drink coffee. He got the coffee maker because it was cheap. It was cheap because it didn't have the carafe that goes with it. Coffee makers are made in such a way that only a certain carafe will work with that maker. He wasn't even sure if it worked. So, here is a worthless coffee maker owned by a man who doesn't drink coffee.

She asked him, "On a scale of one to ten how much pain would it cause you to get rid of this coffee maker."

"About an 8." (This is why hoarders have houses that look like they do.) But, here is the real key. Rather than pressing the point, she looked for something that would cause him less pain to get rid of. What they have found is that if they can get rid of something—anything—good things follow. The key is to make the first small step.

Do you remember the story of Albert Bandura helping people with a fear of snakes? The first step was to set an example, but it didn't end there. The next thing is they had to get people moving in baby steps. They had to walk in the room where the snakes were. The snakes were still behind glass, but at least we were in the same room. Once they were used to that, the snake handlers would pull them out of their cages. Now they were in the same room without anything between the people and the snakes. They stepped closer. They paused. They breathed.

They came to believe that the snakes were not harmful at this close distance. By the way, this raises an interesting question: what does it mean to believe? They may have had an intellectual belief that snakes are not poisonous but that kind of belief could not save them from being paralyzed by the sight of snakes. They had to move. One step at a time—quite literally taking baby steps till they were close enough to touch the snakes.

Then they touched them. Stop. Breathe. Wait. Soon the snakes were draped over their necks. All in about three hours. No PowerPoint. No logic. No information. Just two things: an example (someone else holding the snakes) and action (moving closer to the snakes themselves).

Action is sometimes the result of belief—we act on our belief. Sometimes action is the cause of the belief. Because we hold the snakes, we come to believe that they will not harm us. We don't believe until we take action.

Jesus taught people to take action. Teach like Jesus.

How to persuade a person to put a big, ugly, obnoxious sign in his front yard

Suppose your goal was to persuade a person to put a big, ugly, obnoxious sign in his front yard. How would you do it?

Jonathan Freedman and Scott Fraser published an amazing paper on how they did just that. A researcher, posing as a volunteer, went door to door asking people if they could put a big, ugly, obnoxious sign in their front yard. They even showed them a picture of what it looked like. The picture depicted an attractive house that was barely visible because of the big, ugly, obnoxious sign. The sign read DRIVE CAREFULLY. Not surprisingly, only 17% complied. What to do?

By now, you already know. Get people to take some small baby step in that direction and it will warm them up to do the difficult thing. This is exactly what they did. They had a researcher stop by and ask them to display a three-inch-square sign in the window of their car or home that read, "BE A SAFE DRIVER." It seemed like such a small request, who could resist? It seemed like such a small thing that you wouldn't think it would make much difference, but two weeks later, when the researcher came back and asked permission to put up a big, ugly, obnoxious sign, a whopping 76% of homeowners agreed!

Getting started is the most difficult part of any task. Once we get started, momentum becomes our friend, and that can make a huge difference. Freedman and Fraser explained their results like this:[57]

> *What may occur is a change in the person's feelings about getting involved or taking action. Once he has agreed to a request, his attitude may change, he may become, in his own eyes, the kind of person who does this sort of thing, who agrees to requests made by strangers, who takes action on things he believes in, who cooperates with good causes.*

Sometimes we need to ask for the big order

Baby steps are a great way to begin the process toward total obedience to Christ. It is a great way to start, but we must not stop with baby steps.

Jesus started with baby steps. At first he just said, "Come, follow me." Follow and learn. Listen and discover. Hang out. See what you think.

---

[57] Cialdini, Robert B. (2008-07-29). *Influence* (Kindle Locations 1620-1623). Allyn & Bacon. Kindle Edition.

After a year or so of listening and learning, Jesus turned up the heat:

- *Luke 9:23-26 (NIV) Then he said to them all: "If anyone would come after me, he must deny himself and take up his cross daily and follow me. For whoever wants to save his life will lose it, but whoever loses his life for me will save it. What good is it for a man to gain the whole world, and yet lose or forfeit his very self? If anyone is ashamed of me and my words, the Son of Man will be ashamed of him when he comes in his glory and in the glory of the Father and of the holy angels.*

- *Luke 14:26-27 (NIV) "If anyone comes to me and does not hate his father and mother, his wife and children, his brothers and sisters--yes, even his own life--he cannot be my disciple. And anyone who does not carry his cross and follow me cannot be my disciple.*

- *John 12:25-26 (NIV) The man who loves his life will lose it, while the man who hates his life in this world will keep it for eternal life. Whoever serves me must follow me; and where I am, my servant also will be. My Father will honor the one who serves me.*

- *Matthew 6:24 (NIV) No one can serve two masters. Either he will hate the one and love the other, or he will be devoted to the one and despise the other. You cannot serve both God and Money.*

Many teachers don't ever get around to these kinds of statements. We get stuck in asking for baby steps—if we ask them to do anything at all. We are too timid. We need to ask for the big order. We need to ask men to lay down their lives. We don't merely ask for a little help. We ask them to lay down their lives. Baby steps are a fine way to start. Eventually we must ask people to jump off the cliff.

Winston Churchill knew this. He knew how to make the big ask. He is famously quoted as saying, "I have nothing to offer but blood, toil, tears and sweat."

And how did they respond? All of England rose and said with Churchill, "We will fight in the trenches; we will fight on the beaches. We will never, never, never give up."

Bill Hybels found that people respond favorably with the big ask: [58]

> When handled properly, people are actually quite flattered to be asked to do significant things for God. Granted, they might not always say yes—they can't

---

[58] Hybels, Bill (2008-09-01). *Axiom: Powerful Leadership Proverbs* (Kindle Locations 326-328). Zondervan. Kindle Edition.

always say yes—but they are almost always honored by a wise and well-timed ask.

In the Great Commission Jesus asked us to make disciples of all nations. Now, that is a big ask! In describing what he meant Jesus included the phrase, "teaching to obey. . ." Not merely teaching them to recall everything Jesus had said, but teaching them to obey what Jesus had said to do. We are not out to make smarter sinners. We are out to make saints. We must teach them to obey. We must teach them to do.

Unexpected

Do you serve God for reward?

This is the question the devil asked God in Job 1.9, "Does Job fear God for nothing?"

What is the assumption behind the question? What is the question behind the question? What is the devil thinking?

The assumption is that if Job did not fear God for nothing—if he feared God for what he could get out of it—well, that is not very noble. Job is just being selfish. And that is the question, "Is Job really all that commendable if he fears God for what he gets out of it?"

This is what religious people expect. We expect that it is good to do for others. We don't expect it is good for us to do what is good for us. If you work for your own benefit, we expect there won't be any reward for that.

This is what Immanuel Kant taught. He believed that an action is moral only in that I have no desire to perform it. If I derive some benefit from it, I am just being selfish. If I serve because I am rewarded for service, the service is not a moral act. Piper puts it this way: "Kant loves a disinterested giver. God loves a cheerful giver (2 Cor. 9:7). Disinterested performance of duty displeases God. He wills that we *delight* in doing good and that we do it with the confidence that our obedience secures and increases our joy in God."[59]

There are a lot of things unexpected about Jesus' teaching. This is among the most unexpected: Jesus taught for reward. Jesus appealed to our benefit. He asked us to deny ourselves *so that* we could have Christ; *so that* our life could be saved:

> Then Jesus said to his disciples, "If anyone would come after me, he must deny himself and take up his cross and follow me. For whoever wants to save his life will lose it, but whoever loses his life for me will find it. What good will it be for a man if he gains the whole world, yet forfeits his soul? Or what can a man give in exchange for his soul? For the Son of Man is going to come in his Father's glory with his angels, and then he will reward each person according to what he has done.
> Matthew 16:24-27 (NIV)

---

[59] *Brothers, We Are Not Professionals: A Plea to Pastors for Radical Ministry.* John Piper.

Note that he didn't ask us to deny ourselves and that is that. He didn't ask us to lay down our lives just because. He said that this is the way to really have life. Note the appeal to reward in the last verse above: "he will reward each person according to what he has done."

Reward of prayer

One of the best examples of this appeal to reward is in Jesus' teaching in the Sermon on the Mount. Please allow me to paraphrase and sermonize on this passage:

> Be careful not to do your 'acts of righteousness' before men, to be seen by them. If you do, you will have no reward from your Father in heaven. And what you want is the real reward, right? You don't want to settle for the small reward; you want the big, eternal reward. Here is how you get it. When you give to the needy, do not announce it with trumpets, as the hypocrites do in the synagogues and on the streets, to be honored by men. I tell you the truth, they have received their reward in full. I guarantee that is much less than the reward you will get if you don't go for the reward now. But when you give to the needy, do not let your left hand know what your right hand is doing, so that your giving may be in secret. Then your Father, who sees what is done in secret, will reward you. That is the reward you want; hold out for nothing less.

*And when you pray, do not be like the hypocrites, for
they love to pray standing in the synagogues and on
the street corners to be seen by men. I tell you the truth,
they have received their reward in full. They are settling
for the lesser reward. Don't you do it. When you pray,
go into your room, close the door and pray to your
Father, who is unseen. Then your Father, who sees
what is done in secret, will reward you. Trust me, it will
be good. This is the reward you want. Matthew 6:1-6
(NIV)*

You might fear I was far from solid ground in this
interpretation of the text. You might think I am
taking too much liberty in adding to the words of
Jesus. Consider the words of John Piper:

*Beware of commentators who divert attention from
the plain meaning of these texts. What would you
think, for example, of the following typical comment
on Luke 14:13-14: "The promise of reward for this kind
of life is there as a fact. You do not live this way for the
sake of reward. If you do you are not living in this way
but in the old selfish way."*

*Is this true—that we are selfish and not loving if we
are motivated by the promised reward? If so, why did
Jesus entice us by mentioning the reward, even giving
it as the basis of our action? And what would this
commentator say concerning Luke 12:33, where we are
not told that reward will result from our giving alms,
but we are told to actively seek to get the reward—
"provide yourselves with moneybags"?*

178

And what would he say concerning the Parable of the Unrighteous Steward (Luke 16:1-13), where Jesus concludes, "Make friends for yourselves by means of unrighteous wealth, so that when it fails they may receive you into the eternal dwellings" (16:9)? The aim of this parable is to instruct the disciples in the right and loving use of worldly possessions. Jesus does not say that the result of such use is to receive eternal dwellings. He says to make it your aim to secure an eternal dwelling by the use of your possessions.

So it is simply wrong to say that Jesus does not want us to pursue the reward He promises. He commands us to pursue it (Luke 12:33; 16:9). More than forty times in the Gospel of Luke there are promises of reward and threats of punishment connected with the commands of Jesus.[6][60]

That it may go well with you

Jesus' teaching on the reward of living righteously stands squarely on the shoulders of Old Testament teaching. Nine times in the book of Deuteronomy alone we are told to obey "so that it may go well with you." Here are a few examples. I have highlighted the key phrase:

- Deuteronomy 4:40 (NIV) Keep his decrees and commands, which I am giving you to-day, **so that it may go well with you** and your children after you and that you may live

---

[60] *Desiring God: Meditations of a Christian Hedonist.* John Piper

long in the land the LORD your God gives you for all time.

- Deuteronomy 5:16 (NIV) Honor your father and your mother, as the LORD your God has commanded you, so that you may live long and **that it may go well with you** in the land the LORD your God is giving you.
- Deuteronomy 6:3 (NIV) Hear, O Israel, and be careful to obey **so that it may go well with you** and that you may increase greatly in a land flowing with milk and honey, just as the LORD, the God of your fathers, promised you.
- Deuteronomy 6:18 (NIV) Do what is right and good in the LORD's sight, **so that it may go well with you** and you may go in and take over the good land that the LORD promised on oath to your forefathers,

Better for you

Part of the Sermon on the Mount covers the topic of adultery. Nothing unexpected here: Jesus is against it. In fact, he is even against lust. That is not too unexpected either. He uses rather strong language; he speaks of gouging out your eye and throwing it away. That is a little unexpected language, but then, preachers have been known to get ramped up about sin.

Here is what is unexpected: the reason he gives for avoiding adultery and lust: "It is better for you."

He says it twice. The word means "profitable, advantageous or beneficial." The motive he appeals to is self-interest. He doesn't ask us to deny self-interest. He asks us to maximize self-interest. Religious teachers hardly ever do that. Very unexpected.

Jesus repeats this theme in Matthew 18. Notice again the strong language and notice again the reason Jesus gives for avoiding sin:

> *Matthew 18:8-9 (NIV) If your hand or your foot causes you to sin cut it off and throw it away. It is better for you to enter life maimed or crippled than to have two hands or two feet and be thrown into eternal fire. ⁹And if your eye causes you to sin, gouge it out and throw it away. It is better for you to enter life with one eye than to have two eyes and be thrown into the fire of hell.*

Two more times Jesus says, "It is better for you." It is profitable. It is advantageous. It is beneficial . . . for you.

Jesus was all about what was better for us. He didn't ask us to be good just because or because it would make God happy or glorify God. All those things are true, but expected. What is unexpected is the appeal to self-interest: it will be better for you.

Are the religious happier?

This raises an interesting question, with answers from an unexpected place: science. Are Christians happier?

There is a growing body of scientific research in the field of happiness. For decades psychology studied psychological *illness*. Only recently have scientists begun to study what makes us happy. One of the most predictable findings is that participation in religion tends to do so. Here is Sonja Lyubomirsky:

> Indeed, a growing body of psychological science is suggesting that religious people are happier, healthier, and recover better after traumas than nonreligious people. In one study, parents who had lost a baby to sudden infant death syndrome were interviewed three weeks after their loss and then again after eighteen months. Those who attended religious services frequently and who reported religion as being important to them were better able to cope eighteen months after the loss, showing relatively less depression at this time and greater well-being than nonreligious parents.[61]

---

[61] Lyubomirsky, Sonja (2007-12-27). T*he How of Happiness* (p. 228). Penguin Press Hardcover. Kindle Edition.

Ed Diener:

> *Psychologists who have studied whether religious people are happy or unhappy have often reached a general conclusion - religious people are on the whole happier than the nonreligious. In the vast majority of studies, religious people report higher well-being than their nonbelieving counterparts. Even when researchers define religiosity in various ways - such as attending church or having self-professed spiritual beliefs - studies show that religious people are, on average, mildly happier.[62]*

One more:

> *There is plenty of evidence that people who practice religion enjoy benefits in health and well-being.[63]*

Are Christians happier?

But, science is a pretty blunt instrument when it comes to measuring religion. Science has made little attempt to make distinctions between the religious. There is no attempt to distinguish between real followers and those who are going through the motions.

---

[62] Ed Diener; Robert Biswas-Diener. *Happiness: Unlocking the Mysteries of Psychological Wealth* (Kindle Locations 1470-1472). Kindle Edition.

[63] Daniel Nettle. *Happiness: The Science behind Your Smile* (Kindle Locations 1122-1123). Kindle Edition

So, I did a survey of 1067 of my friends. Now, this isn't a random survey, and it isn't an even cross section of society. My friends are mostly pastors and small group leaders. 48% strongly agree with the statement, "I am totally sold out to Christ. He is absolutely the Lord of my life." This group of people is uniquely suited to helping us make distinctions among committed and more committed Christians. One question I had was, "Are the committed happier?" Turns out they are—a lot happier.

Of those who strongly agreed with the statement, "I am totally sold out to Christ. He is absolutely the Lord of my Life." 28% reported themselves to be extremely happy. For those who agreed (as opposed to strongly agreed) with that statement, the number dropped by two-thirds—11% were extremely happy. Those not sold-out were a grumpy lot. Only 1% reported extreme happiness.

Note: this theme is expanded more fully in my book *Obedience*.

By the way, this group did not just *say* they were sold out. They acted sold out. Four out of five tithe. Three out of five regularly serve God in the area of their gifting. Two-thirds strongly agree with the statement, "I am living a sexually pure life." Nine out of ten love to worship. Three fourths witness regularly. All the things we normally think of committed Christians doing, this group is more likely to do. And, this group is 28 times more likely to be extremely happy when compared with people who describe themselves as not sold out.

Happiness and commitment come together. But, so does happiness and everything else Christ asks us to do. God is a rewarder. For example, God asks us to be generous. Turns out, generous people are happier. In fact, those who describe themselves as very generous are nearly five times as likely to describe themselves as extremely happy. And, this is not merely a subjective evaluation of generosity. If we look at actual giving percentages, the same trend holds true.

What about sexual purity? A lot of people think God is a cosmic kill-joy when it comes to sex. I have a feeling that a lot of people hesitate to come to God because they don't want to follow His plan for sexual purity. Turns out, people who follow God's plan are happier. The sexually pure are four times more likely to be extremely happy.

Let's look at service. We know God has asked us to serve. Pastors regularly ask their people to serve. People tend to resist. The Bible says about Jesus that He came "not to be served but to serve." If we are going to be like Jesus, we will become serving people. Many don't like the idea of serving. They would rather be served. They would rather relax. They would rather be entertained. We have the mistaken notion that serving will make us less happy, not more.

But, the research does not support this. The research clearly indicates that people who serve are happier—much happier. Here was the statement: "I regularly serve God in a way God has gifted me to serve." Thirty percent of those who strongly agreed with that statement were extremely happy—three times the number compared to those who merely agreed with the statement. For those who disagreed—those who said they don't regularly serve God in the way God has gifted them—I could not find any that were extremely happy. No not one, no not one.

Forgiving when it is hard to forgive is another area that is sometimes difficult for us. Jesus commanded us to forgive and tied our own forgiveness with our willingness to forgive others. Forgiveness not only feels difficult at times, it feels impossible.

I made a post recently about this on Facebook. One friend responded to me privately saying she could never forgive a man who had sexually harassed her daughter at work. She was deeply hurt and could not imagine entertaining the possibility of forgiving this one who had violated her daughter. I might feel the same way if it were my daughter. But, the truth is, when we refuse to forgive, we not only cut ourselves off from the forgiveness of God, we also will find ourselves to be substantially less happy.

Here is the statement I had on the survey: "I freely and quickly forgive others when they hurt me." Those who strongly agree with that statement were nearly twelve times more likely to be extremely happy.

I could go on and on. Everything God asks us to do correlates with happiness. Nothing God asks us to do makes us less happy. God asks us to be grateful and grateful people are happier. We are encouraged to read our Bibles and people who do are happier. We are invited to pray and we find that people who pray are happier. We are asked to witness and people who witness are happier.

If you teach people, it is a good idea to keep this in mind as you teach. Appeal to people's self-interest, don't work against it. A statement I try to make often as I teach and write lessons is, "It is always in our best interest to live the Christian life." (For more on my lessons, see www.joshhunt.com)

Jesus said, "I have come that you might have life, and have it to the full." Turns out, those who follow Him most closely are living proof that it is true. It really is good news to all men.

Slogans

I have saved the best for last. This chapter, if applied skillfully, could radically improve how much the people who listen to you remember. Jesus taught using slogans. He reduced complex truth down to memorable slogans. The Bible word is proverb. A slogan is a short, pithy, crisp saying. They stick to the brain like lint on a black suit.

Don't think of Jesus as speaking in proverbs? Check out this verse: "Jesus used this figure of speech, but they did not understand what he was telling them." John 10:6 (NIV)

Notice how the translations treat the phrase, "figure of speech":

- John 10:6 (CEV) Jesus told the people this <u>story</u>. But they did not understand what he was talking about.
- John 10:6 (GW) Jesus used this <u>illustration</u> as he talked to the people, but they didn't understand what he meant.

- John 10:6 (ESV) This **figure of speech** Jesus used with them, but they did not understand what he was saying to them.
- John 10:6 (TEV) Jesus told them this **parable**, but they did not understand what he meant.
- John 10:6 (MSG) Jesus told this **simple story**, but they had no idea what he was talking about.

You might think this is the garden variety word parable, but it is not. It is a work only used five times in the New Testament. Let's look at how this same word is translated in other contexts in the NIV:[64]

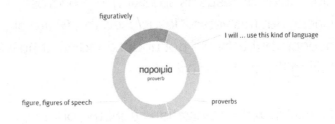

I draw your attention to the time this word is translated proverb. Note also that "proverb" is the basic dictionary definition of the word. (That is what is in the center of the chart.) Here is an

_____

[64] Copyright Faithlife Corporation, makers of Logos Bible Software – www.logos.com

example: "Of them the proverbs are true: 'A dog returns to its vomit,' and, 'A sow that is washed returns to her wallowing in the mud.'" 2 Peter 2.22 NIV

You get a sense for the kind of language that is meant by this word. A proverb. A slogan. A saying. A short, pithy truth-capsule.

Jesus used this kind of language all the time. Here is an example:

- Then you will know the truth, and the truth will set you free. John 8:32 (NIV)

This teaching is quoted by preachers. It is quoted by atheists. It is etched into stone in cathedrals and courthouses and schools. You probably memorized it without trying to memorize it.

Here is another one. See if you can recall what comes after this:

- You are the salt of the earth. Matthew 5:13a (NIV)

Jesus explains himself a bit: "But if the salt loses its saltiness, how can it be made salty again? It is no longer good for anything, except to be thrown out and trampled by men." Matthew 5:13a (NIV) Can you recall what he says next?

- You are the light of the world. Matthew 5:14a (NIV)

It is easy to recall because of the way it is written. Because Jesus reduced it to a slogan, it sticks to the brain. Andy Stanley says, "Memorable is portable." That is, or course, a memorable saying in and of itself. Bruce Wilkinson said, "Don't use paragraphs; use short, punchy sentences."[65] Rick Warren said, "People don't remember sermons or speeches—they don't even remember paragraphs. What people remember are. . . slogans."[66]

A slogan in every lesson

As I write lessons each week, I try to come up with a repeated phrase like this that works its way into half the questions in the lessons. Say I am teaching on faith. I might ask. . .

- What are the advantages for us of being a person of faith and confidence?

---

[65] *The Seven Laws of the Learner: How to Teach Almost Anything to Practically Anyone* by Bruce Wilkinson

[66] Rick Warren, *Purpose Driven Church.*

- What does lack of faith and confidence cost us?
- How do we develop faith and confidence?
- What keeps us from being people of faith and confidence?
- Who has been an example to you of a person of faith and confidence?
- Describe a time when you exhibited faith and confidence.

What phrase do you think will be rolling around the brains of the people I teach come Sunday afternoon?

Here is another example. Suppose I am teaching on forgiving others. I could talk about forgiving others or add a little something to it:

- Why should we forgive when forgiving is difficult?
- Who can tell of a time when you forgave and it was difficult?
- What does it cost us when we don't forgive when forgiving is difficult?
- How do we find the grace to forgive when forgiving is difficult?

Here is one more example of a slogan—this one from the mouth of Jesus. See if you can complete this verse: Matthew 7:12 (NIV) So in everything, do to others what you would _____ _____." Get it? Do you remember when you memorized this verse? You likely didn't have to because of the way Jesus said it. It is just so sticky.

A lesson from science

A good slogan can create the perception that something exists when there is no scientific evidence that it does. Case in point: road rage. In 1994 no one had heard of road rage. Then people started talking. The phrase was so catchy it was easy to pass along. In 1995, the phrase started to multiply in the media, and by 1996 the issue had become a serious public concern.[67] California gave it legal status.[68] It seems everyone was concerned with road rage. Funny thing about road rage—it didn't exist. It was a figment of our collective imagination. It was kindled by the fact that the term "road rage" was just so darn catchy and was fanned into flames by the media. But the best science we have on the subject reveals there never was a road rage epidemic. Sure, there were crazies on the road, but there have always been crazies on the road. There was no evidence

---

[67] Gardner, Daniel (2008-07-17). *The Science of Fear: How the Culture of Fear Manipulates Your Brain* (p. 177). Plume. Kindle Edition.

[68] http://en.wikipedia.org/wiki/Road_rage

whatsoever of an increase in actual road rage. Here is what the research revealed:[69]

> When panics pass, they are simply forgotten, and where they came from and why they disappeared are rarely discussed in the media that featured them so prominently. If the road-rage panic were to be subjected to such an examination, it might reasonably be suggested that its rise and fall simply reflected the reality on American roads. But the evidence doesn't support that. "Headlines notwithstanding, there was not—there is not—the least statistical or other scientific evidence of more aggressive driving on our nation's roads," concluded journalist Michael Fumento in a detailed examination of the alleged epidemic published in The Atlantic Monthly in August 1998. "Indeed, accident, fatality and injury rates have been edging down. There is no evidence that 'road rage' or an aggressive-driving 'epidemic' is anything but a media invention, inspired primarily by something as simple as alliteration: road rage."

So, why was there widespread public perception that road rage was rampant? Much of it was the phrase was so easy to say. It was just too fun to talk about road rage. Ideas spread when we reduce them to a slogan.

---

[69] Gardner, Daniel (2008-07-17). *The Science of Fear: How the Culture of Fear Manipulates Your Brain* (p. 177). Plume. Kindle Edition

Lessons from history

What did this man say to this crowd on this day?

Do you know how many times Martin Luther King Jr. repeated that phrase, "I have a dream" in his famous 1963 speech on the Washington Mall? Nine times.

What did this man say to this crowd on this day?

As I see the picture I can hear that Massachusetts accent, "Ask not what your country can do for you; ask what you can do for your country." Spoken as a true democrat. Bring back those democrats. I never tried to memorize that line. I couldn't keep from memorizing that line because Kennedy said it in such a memorable way.

What do you recall that this man said?

42.
Bill Clinton 1993-2001

It always gets a chuckle when I ask this to live audiences. The one I remember is, "I did not have sex with that woman!"

Lessons from sermons

I recall a sermon I heard forty years ago. Forty years ago. The title was "One more night with the frogs." The story was Pharaoh and Moses and the story of the ten plagues. This one was frogs. Frogs everywhere. Frogs in the bed. Frogs in the sofa. Frogs in the dishes. Frogs in the toilet. Finally, Pharaoh can't stand it any longer and he demands Moses get rid of the frogs. Moses says, "Fine, when would you like the frogs to go?"

Pause.

How would you answer that question? When? Yesterday! Right now! As soon as possible! Now! ASAP! How does Pharaoh respond? "First thing tomorrow morning." One more night with the frogs.

Why did he say tomorrow morning? Because we all like to be large and in charge. We like to play tough. We like to think we can take it.

Talk to a man about what a mess his life is and how he needs Christ. "It's not that bad," he will say. How bad does it have to be?

Talk to a man about coming to Christ and you are more likely to hear, "Not now," than "Never." One more night with the frogs.

What keeps more people from Christ than any other single thing? Procrastination. One more night with the frogs.

I remember all of that from a sermon forty years ago because the preacher, Bill Tisdale, reduced it to a slogan: One more night with the frogs.

Can you recall a sermon R. G. Lee preached? I ask this question before groups and they can always come up with the answer: Payday Someday.

Can you recall a sermon that Jonathan Edwards preached? How about, "Sinners in the hands of an angry God."

Jesus used slogans all the time. Teach like Jesus.

Conclusion

I wish I could spend a day with Jesus. I wish I could watch Jesus deliver just one talk. I wish I could hear the tone of his voice. I wish I was born in the language he was speaking. I wish I could watch if he stood or sat. Did he walk among the crowd? Did he stand on the stage? What was his eye contact like? Did he ever touch people when he taught? Did he ever use notes? Did he stand behind a lectern?

If Jesus were living in the flesh today would he use PowerPoint? Would he speak more often in churches, at restaurants, in homes, or in some other public hall? Would he enhance his teaching with video? Would he want dramatic stage lighting? Would he have his disciples set up really cool stage décor?

Doing this study has raised more questions for me than it has answered. The more I have learned the more curious I have become. I hope you have become curious too. I hope you disagree with me at times. I hope you read the gospels in a whole different way — looking for how Jesus taught, not merely what Jesus taught.

There is a lot to learn. This is only the beginning. Learn to teach like Jesus.

Made in the USA
Monee, IL
18 July 2024

62073335R00128